# ATTRACTING
# FEEDING & HOUSING
# WILD BIRDS
## WITH PROJECT PLANS

### PHYLLIS MOORMAN

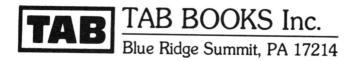

TAB BOOKS Inc.

Blue Ridge Summit, PA 17214

FIRST EDITION

FIRST PRINTING

Copyright © 1985 by TAB BOOKS Inc.

Printed in the United States of America

Library of Congress Cataloging in Publication Data

Moorman, Phyllis.
    Attracting, feeding, and housing wild birds--with project plans.

    Includes index.
    1. Birds, Attracting of. I. Title.
QL676.5.M66   1985       639.9′78       84-26893
ISBN 0-8306-0755-2
ISBN 0-8306-1755-8 (pbk.)

Cover photograph: The National Audubon Society Collection/PR.

# Contents

# Preface

I'm one of those people who enjoys hearing the chatter of birds in the morning. Right now, as I write, I am half-listening to a mockingbird going through his entire repertoire in the oaks outside. One of my neighbors complains about this particular bird because he occasionally sings way before dawn. I've lain awake many a moonlit night and listened to him. I think it's beautiful. That's the main difference between us. My neighbor won't be interested in this book. But, if you enjoy the peace and beauty that birds can lend to your garden, and if you enjoy the endless variety and the never-ending antics they bring, I wrote this book for you.

# Acknowledgments

Of course, my acknowledgments have to go to my family: to my husband, who was my critic and prod, and to my three children, who heard a thousand times, "Don't bother Mommy, she's working on the book."

# Introduction

The boom is on. You can walk into just about any type of store, from supermarket to garden shop, and find bird feeders and houses in a bewildering variety of styles. More people than ever before are buying them, indicating more interest than ever before in attracting birds. Yet, while there are many attractive "coffee table" type books or research tomes available, there are very few recent books on the shelves that touch on the practical aspects of attracting wild birds to your property. When it is possible to find one that details construction of feeders and birdhouses, too many times it is outdated when it comes to methods and materials. Or often it is simply a book of design plans, one after another, with no broad look at building a system or environment to attract the most birds. After all, it does little good to build a lovely feeder and then not know the ins and outs of locating and stocking it.

This book offers both proven methods and designs and a thorough, updated overview of the hobby. Materials are modern and easy to acquire in an urban or suburban setting. Discussions of feeding methods and foods are taken from recent research and changes in availability and convenience of different food items. The reader should find this book to be a "bible" of information on attracting, feeding, and housing wild birds.

# Chapter 1

# Attracting Birds

IT STANDS TO REASON THAT IF YOU HAVE OPENED THIS BOOK
you have at least a passing interest in birds. Maybe you have
become interested in the ones you have been seeing in your yard,
or maybe you are an old pro who has been a bird hobbyist for years.
No matter how you got started, you have become a member of one
of the most popular hobbies in the United States.

## PEOPLE AND BIRDS

Today more people than ever before are involved in attracting,
feeding, and housing the wild birds that live around them. It is
a pastime that allows as much or as little time and participation
as an individual has to spare. You can choose to simply put up a
few houses or to only maintain a small winter feeding program,
or you can take a total environment approach with year-round
feeding and housing, water sources, and protection from birds'
enemies. You might enjoy joining one of the thousands of local bird
enthusiasts' clubs where you can share ideas and experiences with
other people who have the same interests. Whatever level of involvement you want is possible.

### A Popular Hobby

A recent government study estimated that across the country
nearly 39 percent of adults feed wild birds. That is more than one

1

in three! I was surprised to find that there are so many of us. I knew, of course, that on about every block you can find someone feeding birds, from those who just throw out bread scraps to those with one or more elaborate feeders. I know also that we have both a large and active nationally affiliated bird-watchers' club as well as a strictly local one just in our small town. With bird hobbyists being as low-key as they are, I was surprised by that statistic.

To get a better idea of how many bird enthusiasts there are, I called the owner of one local feed store near my home and asked him to estimate how much bird food he sells to hobbyists each week. His figure came to approximately 3000 pounds! That is just one feed store out of several nearby. It does not take into consideration how much the other feed stores sell or how much feed is bought at grocery, variety, and discount stores. Of course it cannot take into account the numbers of people who feed their birds kitchen scraps or raise natural foods for them.

Another way to get a picture of the large number of people interested in wild birds is to recall how many commercially available bird houses and feeders there are on the market now. In nearly every nursery, discount store, garden shop, pet store, or variety store you will find a selection of plastic prefab or kitted houses and feeders. Manufacturers of these products say they are selling better than ever before.

Once you start looking, you will begin to notice more bird enthusiasts than you imagined. In fact, I can walk around my own block and find two other enthusiasts in that short distance. I have met both of them, and they are pretty much representative. One is an older woman who has lived in this region all of her life. She knows the birds around her by their common names and, in some cases, by country nicknames I had not heard before. Everything she knows about the local birds' diets and habits she has learned by word of mouth or by her own observation. When I have a question the field guides and reference books cannot answer, she is a big help. This woman keeps two feeders stocked all year, and she has several birdhouses of various types scattered over her property.

Up the street in the other direction are other local cohorts in the bird attracting hobby. They are more comfortable with a scientific approach. The wife keeps a field guide, binoculars, and logbook handy to jot down new species sighted. The two children keep the feeders filled and can tell as much about various birds' ranges, diets, and nesting habits as most adults. The landscaping in their yard has been carefully planned and planted so as to include plants that provide the best shelter, nesting sites, and natural foods. The whole family is interested in birds and the environment to the extent that they belong to several national conservation orgnizations.

Whether you fit into one of the above patterns or not, you will find about every type of people imaginable involved in attracting, feeding, and housing wild birds.

## It Is Enjoyable and Necessary

As our urban and suburban areas grow and overtake forest and farmlands where birds have always lived, whole habitants are changed or destroyed. Trees, bushes, and other plants are cut down that were the nesting sites, shelter, and food supplies of dozens of species. The ever closer proximity of people, their animals, and their vehicles moves some species completely out of the area. Then they have to compete with other birds for food and territory. Pollution makes it harder to find pure water and untainted food. Even in the less built-in areas zealous gardeners are careful to chop away old dead limbs from their trees, inadvertently depriving hole-nesting birds of their natural homes. Vacant lots are cleared, marshes are drained, and brush is cleared, taking away the bits of habitat left to the birds.

Many bird species have learned to adjust, at least somewhat, to these habitat changes. Sparrows and doves, in some areas, have become almost as bold as pets. Wrens and flickers have learned to nest in birdhouses as have many other species. More and more species are becoming regular visitors at urban and suburban feeders, supplementing their dwindling natural food supply with food that man furnishes. Water is often more of a problem, especially in summer, where many types of birds depend on lawn sprinklers and gutter puddles for their needs. I have seen jays and sparrows who have become incredibly adept at clinging upside down to a water faucet to catch an occasional drop of water. Many of the species are adapting instead of moving off to new territories or dying out. The point remains, though, that it has become a struggle for many species of birds to survive in what were once their natural habitats. This makes it important, in my view, for people to do what they can to help; on a national scale by working for a better environment, on a local scale by working for things like bird sanctuaries and green belts, and on a personal level by helping to provide new sources of water, food, nesting sites, and shelter.

Along with the diminishing natural habitats, birds also face an age-old danger that concerned bird hobbyists can lessen—winter.

Every year winter cold and exposure kills more birds than anything else. Only the strongest and fittest birds can last a season outside in the bitter weather, and even some of those that migrate are so weakened by their long trip that they succumb to winter, too.

Nature has provided a complex energy management system for birds' survival in winter. First, their covering of feathers acts as variable insulation. On warmer days, you will see the birds keeping their feathers sleek and flat. When it is colder, they will fluff them out, creating more of an "insulation blanket" to trap warm, body-heated air around them. The structure of birds' legs is designed for energy conservation, too. The legs consist mostly of bone and connective tissue. They are thinly fleshed, without much for the birds to have to nourish and keep warm.When they perch, birds flex their legs and, in effect, sit down over their bent legs, covering them with their downy feathers. These factors, along with their specialized circulatory systems capable of a semihibernation called *torpidity*,, help birds survive the cold.

Even with all these clever adaptations, many birds still die from exposure and cold. The fast metabolic rate necessary to maintain enough body heat during cold weather requires very frequent intake of food since the birds cannot store enough in their crops to last a whole day. This, in turn, makes finding enough food even more critical in the winter. Not only is food scarce and the weather bad, but the need is greater. The constant need to find food is the reason you will find birds out foraging in the very worst weather.

Like the problem of habitat loss, the effects of winter on local bird populations can be lessened by concerned individuals. It only takes a minimal amount of expense to build a few shelter boxes and birdhouses of scrap lumber and to provide kitchen scraps as a food supply. Most of us in the hobby feel a responsibility for wild birds. We know we are not only doing something that we enjoy, but we are also helping them to survive.

## WHAT IS REQUIRED TO ATTRACT BIRDS?

If you want birds to visit your property, you must give them a reason to come. Even before you start your actual feeding and housing program, you might have had a yard that just naturally attracted birds. If you have dense trees and shrubbery for shelter and nesting, an area of uncleared brush, plants that provide fruit, seeds, or berries, or a water source, you already have some regular bird visitors. You can increase the number of birds that come by making the total environment even more attractive.

In general, it takes more than a helter-skelter approach to attract the maximum number of birds. Just throwing out kitchen scraps as they accumulate will certainly draw bird visitors but not as many as a regularly-stocked feeder will. By the same token, planting cover plants and trees will attract nesting birds but not as many as a few good bird houses will. What you should aim for is the creation of a total environment that will make birds feel at home and secure.

Creating this kind of environment is not as troublesome as it may seem. Essentially, it means providing a few basic requirements, as listed below, and doing what you can to make your yard a safe haven from cats, dogs, mischievous children, and other hazards. Once the local and migrating birds get used to the physical layout of your yard and the fact that they will not be molested there, more and more will appear. For now let's take a brief look at these basic requirements. There is a complete section on each later in the book (Chapters 4 and 5), but seeing them together as a unit gives a nice overview of what is necessary in the environment.

## Food

For most people who begin attracting birds, providing food is the first step. Many of them start out with scrap feeding or with a small, commercial feeder and a commercial seed mix. Actually, as you get more and more into the hobby, you will discover more options from various seed mixtures to suet to planting natural food sources. Further reading in this book and others will give you a good idea of which foods will be within your budget, easy for you to store and handle, and attractive to the birds you have around you. You can also begin by first learning the preferred diets of birds you especially like and providing those foods in hopes of bringing them to your yard.

Of all the basic requirements for attracting birds and creating the proper environment, I think I would have to place providing food as the most important. A water source or nesting sites will certainly draw birds but not a fraction as fast as birds are attracted to a steady food supply. Providing food is the basic groundwork under your whole system. Once the birds become regular visitors in search of food, they will use your waterers, stay around enough to take advantage of the cover plants or brush piles you provide, and discover your birdhouses.

## Water

Since many birds have to travel long distances from their feeding and nesting sites each day to find water, having a source of it in your yard is a sure bet for attracting them. You will also enjoy watching the antics of the different birds as they splash and play in it. Waterers of any type pay dividends in the numbers of birds and in the enjoyment you will have.

## Shelter and Cover

Shelter and cover are actually two distinct requirements. I use the term shelter to mean places that offer birds protection from severe weather or protected places to nest. Wintering boxes, bird houses, nesting shelves, and dense evergreens are good shelter. Cover, on the other hand, is used as temporary resting and hiding places. Trees and bushes near your feeder that birds can flit to to avoid enemies are cover. Brush piles that afford a network of hiding places are excellent cover. Tall plants and grasses serve as cover for many types of birds.

As you can see from reading the list, providing cover and shelter takes a little planning and effort. You must build or buy bird houses and arrange to plant cover plants if your yard has none. Even so, it is a requirement that should not be overlooked in providing the best possible environment. Just take a good survey of your yard, noting any cover and shelter you already have, and plan your additions from there. Chapters 5 through 8 detail using landscaping to provide cover and shelter and construction of various kinds of shelter, too.

## Nesting Materials

Making nesting materials available is another of the simple-to-provide requirements that will attract birds for you. It is easy to overlook the difficulty birds have in finding enough of the proper materials for their nests. Birds spend hours and days searching for the right materials, and having a good source in your yard is a good way to help them and encourage them to consider nesting nearby.

## Dust and Grit

While not a critical requirement, your total environment should include dust for dust bathing unless you live in a sandy or dusty area of the country. Some grit birds can ingest to help them break down their food is helpful, too.

## IDENTIFYING AND LEARNING ABOUT YOUR VISITORS

Learning to identify even the most common of your bird visitors can add a great deal to your enjoyment. Although you are probably already familiar with most of the types of birds that visit your yard, as you begin to attract more birds and spend more time observing them, you will see some that are unfamiliar to you. They might be birds that have stopped by during migration or local birds that hadn't visited your yard until now. Often, too, more experienced observation shows individual differences in birds you used to lump together into the same group. For most of us, these unfamiliar birds are a challenge to our curiosities, and learning about them becomes an important part of the hobby.

Identifying your bird visitors does more than satisfy your curiosity, however. It is also important in helping you put together an environment that will encourage them to stay or attract more of the same type. You learn the feeding and nesting habits of the birds, what kind of foods they prefer, and what kind of shelter to provide for them. You will learn which species are common in your area and which ones you can expect to stop through during migrations. Putting all this information together will help you know how to attract the maximum number of birds.

When it comes to actually learning about the birds, you have a large number of resources. The most common one is the use of field guides as I will discuss below. Aside from that, however, the local public library is invaluable. Often there are large, expensive, detailed books there for use that are prohibitively expensive to the amateur. Many times I have found an obscure fact that had baffled me in a library resource book when all my other attempts had failed.

People are another important source of advice and information. Once you get a little bit acquainted, you will be amazed at the number of people around even a small town who can answer most of your questions. If you have a college or junior college nearby, many instructors don't mind answering questions. I always add the caution that these people are busy professionals and should not be bothered with questions that can be answered by any reference book. Save the pros for the really tricky questions. Experienced bird watchers and feeders are another great source of practical information. Here is where to get the scoop on which seeds are preferred by which local species, how high the neighborhood bluebirds prefer to nest, which kind of waterer works best, etc. They can also offer advice on where to find the best prices on bird foods or even where to find some piece of equipment or special type of seed you have not been able to locate. I have met only a very, very few birders who were not delighted to meet and swap stories and advice with another one. For most of us, comparing lists of species sighted, bird tallies, etc., is a great part of the hobby itself. Take advantage of the experience and knowledge available here.

Many bird hobbyists join local bird watching or conservation clubs. This can be a wonderful way to meet people with similar interests. It is also a great way to take advantage of the information, advice, and experience that many member of organizations like this can offer. If you ask at the feed or pet store where you buy your bird food and supplies and scan the newspaper for meeting announcements, you are sure to get in contact with the club near you. In addition to the opportunities for establishing friendships and gleaning information, most bird enthusiasts' clubs sponsor field trips, bird watching expeditions, informative lectures and films, and even bird censuses. If you enjoy meeting people and sharing interests, look up your local club.

These sources of information should get you started in the learning process. As you set up your bird attracting environment and more birds begin to visit, you might find that a few basic pieces of equipment will help you get the most from your observation.

**Field Guides**

As a handy, quick reference, you will find a good field guide is worth its weight in gold. Like most serious bird watchers, I keep mine handy on the windowsill or nearby table where it is in easy reach if I see an unusual bird on one of the feeders or houses. Then I can skim through the pages and usually arrive at an identification. Most good guides also give brief descriptions of the diets, nesting habits, range of the species, and any notable facts about its habits or song. All in all, I would consider a good field guide the most important single reference you could buy.

When you look for a field guide, comparison shopping is a must. There are many, many guides on the market—some very good, many mediocre, and some terrible. Look for reputable names and good quality. I haven't seen a single inexpensive guide that has been good. Most of the good ones run in the $9 to $20 range. It is a good investment.

No matter which field guide you finally settle on, there are a few main features to look for. Be sure, for example, that it contains good, clear photographs instead of drawings. I know some bird experts recommend drawings or water colors for their trueness of color, but I personally haven't been satisfied with anything but color photos. The text of your guide should be clearly written and concise. The technical words and phrases should be explained either in the text or in a glossary-type section. It is handy if the guide shows pictures of both sexes of species where there is great difference in the coloration. An index is worthwhile for those times when you know the name of the bird and want to look at the photo or read the text without thumbing through the identification section. On the information side, you will want one that packs as many useful facts into its small, portable size as possible. I said useful facts, because you will have to read through a few passages to see if the guide tells you what you need to know about the birds you see. For instance, I was once given a copy of a much-touted, nifty little guide complete with a leatherette field cover that I have never carried with me or used much at home. The illustrations are lovely, but the pages that I would prefer to have cover the diet, range, flight characteristics, nesting habits, and juvenile coloration are taken up by a discussion of the evolution of birds and an in-detail discussion of bird family classification. This is not to say I am not interested in these two areas of information, but rather to suggest that, for me, a field guide should be a compact, easily-carried concise compendium of *practical* facts about the bird at the other end of my binoculars. For the rest I will read a reference book at my leisure.

Most field guides are organized to help you locate an unknown bird by noting its color or other distinguishing feature. For example, if your field guide is set up by color, to identify a small greenish yellow bird, you would thumb directly to the appropriate section where all the greenish birds, regardless of size and family, are shown. If you locate your stranger in this section, a caption to the picture refers you to the text, sometimes on an adjacent page or sometimes a wholly separate section, where you could read about it. In other guides, birds are grouped by other characteristics, such as beak and foot shapes or by size or family. No matter how they are arranged, most guides are set up for quick field reference. The idea is for you to be able to make a quick observation, note a basic characteristic or two, and swiftly use the guide for an on-the-spot I.D. Although my personal preference is for the grouping-by-color method of guide arrangement, it is important that you take the time to look any guide you are considering over carefully. Be certain it offers the information you are going to want to have. Check that the illustrations are satisfactory to you. Most important of all, try using it. Take the time, even in the book store, to figure out the steps necessary to efficiently locate a certain bird's photograph and the text that goes with it. Once you try a couple of different guides, you will see just how much they vary in ease of use.

## Binoculars

As more and more birds begin to visit your yard and you begin to watch their antics with a little more interest, you will find that you often cannot see all that you would like to with merely your naked eye. Birds far away across the yard or on a high branch will be hard to identify positively. It will be difficult to closely observe shy or nesting birds, because as you approach, they fly off. When this happens, or if you enjoy going into the field to watch birds, you will begin to see the need for a pair of binoculars.

I keep my binoculars handy. I have one pair near the window from which I usually watch the birds that visit and another in our van for field sightings. Since many times the bird I see will not stay visible long enough for more than just the quickest observation, I want them right there where I can grab them in an instant. You will probably find some convenient station for yours, too, so they will be ready when you need them.

Buying a pair of binoculars means an investment of $35 to over $100 depending on the type and quality you choose, so it makes sense to take care in making your selection. At first you might think you want the most magnification available in your price range. You want to really get a close look at the birds, right? Actually, it doesn't work that way. As you increase the magnification, you increase the need for very steady hands to hold them. The higher powered binoculars are so sensitive to any movement of your hand and arm as to be nearly useless to most novices. The most commonly recommended strength for general field work is 7 or 8 power. Later, after you have gained experience and can handle them, a pair of 10-power binoculars might be useful.

Another factor to consider is the diameter of the front, or objective, lens. This determines how much light is let into the binoculars, which has a great deal to do with how good a "picture" you will be able to see. As a general rule, look for binoculars with an objective diameter of at least five times the magnification. For example, your 7-power binoculars should have an objective size of at least 35 millimeters, and a pair of 8-power glasses should have an objective size of at least 40 millimeters. This relative size comparison should explain why you see designations like $7 \times 35$ or $8 \times 40$ on binoculars. It is a handy way to describe it. If you choose, you can get binoculars with very large objectives. These are good if you expect to do most of your observations in dim light where it is important to have glasses that will let in as much light as possible. You will find, however, that these will allow in too much light and glare. In addition, since the lenses are larger, they are heavier.

Weight has to be a consideration when you make your choice. Often, when you are watching nesting behavior or just trying to classify a stranger on the feeder, you will use the binoculars for five minutes or longer at a single stretch. The heavier they are, the more they waver as you begin to tire. On long field observations you end up propping them against your knee, a branch, or anything else handy. Even just carrying them around cased in the field calls for the lightest possible useful glasses. Since choices of construction materials as well as the size of the lenses factor into the final weight, compare equal power glasses by different manufacturers. You want one constructed ruggedly, able to take the occasional bumps and knocks, but also as light as possible.

There are a few other features to consider, too, for ease of use and practicality. Binoculars are available with coated lenses that act to cut down glare. You will want an adjustable right eyepiece so you can tailor the focus to your own vision. Central focusing allows quick, often one-handed adjustment from viewing far to nearby birds. Zoom features are available on some binoculars that really bring the viewing up close. Your best bet is to shop carefully, comparing features, quality, weight, strength, etc., and then buy the best pair your budget will allow. They should last you many years, so consider spending a little more for features you will be happy with. You can usually get some very good deals on used binoculars by checking the classifieds, yard sales, and pawn shops.

### Cameras

Many people add to their enjoyment of attracting birds by taking photographs of them. The range of possibilities is wide, from simple identification photos for keeping a record of species seen from year to year, to high-interest action photos of flight, nesting activities, etc. For most types of bird photography it takes more than your family 110 or instant camera. A 35mm setup is a good start, and most serious bird and wildlife photographers have a wide range of lenses, tripods, and other specialized equipment that allows them to take wonderful shots of quick-moving and often elusive birds. My own idea of a basic home setup for photographing birds you attract is a good 35mm camera with a zoom lens mounted on an adjustable tripod in front of the window you most commonly view birds from. This way it is sturdily mounted and ready for you to swivel it into position and shoot. Your local camera club, bird-watchers' club, or camera shot can give you advice on equipment, cost, and technique.

## Telescopes

As their interest grows, many people feel the limitations of their binoculars and buy a telescope or spotting scope. A scope enables viewing of birds from longer distances, and since they are usually sturdily mounted on gunstock-like handles or on adjustable tripods, the weight of the larger lenses and the sensitivity caused by the larger objective diameter are not likely to be problems.

When it comes to choosing a scope, keep in mind most of the same considerations as you did for choosing a pair of binoculars. In general, buy the best you can afford; one that you will be satisfied with for several years. Look for an adjustable eyepiece, coated lenses if you prefer them, an objective large enough to let in plenty of light for bright, clear viewing, and sufficient magnification. Although spotting scopes and telescopes are available in strengths up to 60 power and more, I would not suggest anything more than 30 or, at the most, 40 for normal field and home use. Above this strength, the scopes become so sensitive to minute movements and wind vibrations that often the subject being viewed has a trembling, shimmering appearance. A zoom feature is available on many spotting scopes and can be very handy. And, as with binoculars, don't overlook the possibility of saving money on a good one by buying it used.

## Record Books

Most serious bird hobbyists keep some form of record or log

book. In it they note species and numbers of birds sighted, where the sightings took place, the date, conditions, and any other pertinent information. Some are so faithful in their record keeping that they can use the information to compare sightings and other facts from year to year or to share with other hobbyists.

You might find it handy to keep some form of log, too. It doesn't have to be anything formal or difficult to maintain. I first started keeping one simply to satisfy my own curiosity as to how many species of bird were visiting my feeder one winter. I pulled out a spiral notebook and wrote down each new species as I noticed it. After a while I began noting the date, just for reference, and the time of day, because it began to look as though some birds preferred to feed at certain times. In other words, I tailored my record keeping to what interested me about my particular bird population. I still keep the log on a casual basis just noting items of interest like unusual birds or behaviors, numbers of migratory birds that visit from year to year, and when the migratory species arrive and leave. As you get your bird attracting environment set up, you might see the need for your own system, too.

## A Reference Library

Once your curiosity gets aroused by seeing certain birds or behaviors that you cannot identify or explain, you will hit the books if you are like most of us. I have already noted some very good sources of information, such as experienced hobbyists and the public library near you, but sometimes there is no substitute for having information available at your fingertips. After all, at 8 P.M. on a Sunday night you might not want to make a phone call and the library might be closed. A few well-selected books on your shelf pay for themselves very quickly in terms of convenience.

Although many of the most learned texts on ornithology are large, expensive volumes or sets that are too expensive for the average home library, there are many very good general references available. The problem you will often run into in trying to find good ones is that there aren't too many on your neighborhood bookstore's shelves. Since they appeal to a limited market, most stores simply don't carry more than a representative sampling. If you live in a big city where there are specialty bookshops, count yourself fortunate. For the rest of us, I have to recommend mail order.

You will find advertisements for mail order books on every phase of ornithology in most of the nature-oriented magazines. You will also be treated to book reviews in most of them. Read the reviews and the ads as carefully as you can to determine if the contents of the book are really what you are looking for. For example, when I first started out, I looked for ads that specifically pointed out the number and type of illustrations. If a book said "108 beautiful color photos," that was a selling point to me. Now, however, my needs have changed, and I look for text. I look for ads that show a low proportion of illustrations to number of pages of text, and I also want more specific information rather than broad overviews of bird evolution and specialization. Use the ads to help you to choose a helpful reference book. Order it, and once you get it, be prepared to use the usual trial period and send it back if you decide it won't be a good addition to your library.

## Summing Up

Although none of the items and equipment discussed above is essential to the hobby of attracting birds, each one has something to contribute. You will find that one of the things that makes it such a versatile and popular hobby is the way each individual can adapt it to his own particular interests and circumstances. You might be one of us who started out simply and then just sort of escalated, adding a new birdhouse here and a pair of binoculars or a reference book there, until all of a sudden you find yourself a full-fledged bird hobbyist.

# Chapter 2

# Feeding Birds

**F** EEDING BIRDS IS EASY, INEXPENSIVE, AND A HOBBY THAT can give back much more—in the form of enjoyment—than you are required to expend. Many people think of bird feeding as a winter activity only. Extending bird feeding to year-round can increase the variety of birds you see and encourage birds to nest in your yard and use your birdhouses.

There is a catch; that is, feeding, especially winter feeding, is a responsibility. Once you start feeding birds and they become dependent on you for a food supply, you must continue to provide that food source. This point is very important. Many people buy feeders as spur-of-the-moment acts of kindness, keep them filled for a few weeks, and then as interest wanes, they let them stand empty. This is actually an inadvertent cruelty. Food supply is a major factor in a bird's choice of a wintering spot, and this kind of short-term abundance of food can cause suffering to birds when the food runs out.

As you set up your feeding program, you will quickly see just how fast birds do come to depend on you. In a very short while, you will find that if you don't get the feeder filled on time, you will have a bunch of hungry birds perched out in the cold. Or worse, you will find that your early morning visitors have given up and gone elsewhere to find food, which might be a tough assignment unless you are fortunate enough to live in a neighborhood like mine with many feeders. Even then, I know that while not actually very territorial about feeders, flocks of birds do not welcome strangers. Often, newcomers are subjected to a lot of screeching, bluffing, and threats as they try to feed. This is just a temporary, one morning food shortage! Imagine how hard it is for a whole flock of birds who have been dependent upon a feeder for several weeks to suddenly be left without their food source. Those birds probably based their decision to winter in that specific area because there was plenty of food available, and it is too late for them to migrate. It makes for a long, tough winter unless there is another kind person around nearby.

The increased interest in the ecology and conservation has caused more people than ever before to participate in some form of bird feeding program. This has made many birds, whole colonies in some places, absolutely dependent upon man's feeders for winter survival. It has also altered birds natural migration patterns. Bird species that used to migrate south in the fall now winter in many areas. They are totally dependent on the man-furnished food supply that has become available over the years. In some areas, birds are so dependent upon artificial food supplies that it is nearly impossible to find them except in the vicinity of feeders. A few species, such as titmice, are actually increasing their range *north* due to the food available at feeders. Some scientists are concerned about the effects of this dependence. They worry that if someday man's additions to the natural food supply ends, it will mean starvation for vast numbers of birds.

I specified that winter feeding is a special responsibility, and, of course, it is. Food supply often decides winter survival. If you choose to feed through the rest of the year, you should view that as a responsibility, too. Your rewards will be well worth it.

## FEEDING THROUGH THE YEAR

Different seasons mean different requirements for the birds in your yard. Variations in the natural food supply and weather-related energy needs call for changes in the foods supplied in the outdoor feeder. Let's look at each season and what we should provide during each one.

### Fall

You will want to begin feeding early in the fall to catch migrating birds that are passing through. As I said earlier, an abundant food supply is one determining factor in birds' selection of a place to winter. If they pass through your yard and find a steady, reliable food supply, they might easily decide to stay on. If you wait too late in the year to begin, many of these birds, and the local ones too, might be gone. The first part of September is not too early to start in the north for fall feeding, and October is a good time to start in the south. Be sure to establish your yard as a good environment for birds to winter. You will want to provide cover, shelter, water, and a sense of security from harm if you want a large number of birds.

Natural foods at this time of the year are seeds, nuts, and dried flower pods in addition to insects that might still be left. The food you supply can be essentially the same as a winter food without so much emphasis on the high-energy fats so necessary in the dead of winter.

## Winter

I cannot stress the importance of winter feeding enough. Every year many, many birds die from exposure due to a lack of food. With their terrifically high metabolic rate, birds simply must have a constant supply of high-energy foods in the winter. They have to be able to eat several times a day to keep themselves going. In between the times they eat, they digest food that has been stored in their crops. This constant intake is all that is between them and death from exposure. In fact, the balance is so critical that at night-time when hunting food becomes impossible and the temperature drops many species of birds go into a semihibernation called *torpidity* to conserve energy. While torpid, the bird's feet and legs lock into position to keep him on the perch and all his bodily functions slow down—heart rate, respiration, every function. This allows conservation of precious energy during this time when it is not possible to eat. Even with this marvelous capacity, after a particularly cold night, you will see dead, frozen birds on the ground under the trees they perched in. Not even torpidity is total protection. The survivors awaken early in the morning and must seek food as quickly as possible. This is one reason why you will always see birds out in any but the absolute worst weather. They must search for food.

If you have started feeding early in the fall, you will have a large clientele by this time. You will know who are your early morning and late afternoon visitors and who comes and goes all day long. You will have a good handle on which foods are preferred by which species and how much to provide. You will be committed to keeping the feeders supplied all winter even while you are away on vacation.

Natural foods will be getting scarcer and scarcer now, and the normal supplies of holleyberries, cedar berries, barberries, and crabapples will be gone as well as most of the seeds from trees like ash, birch, maple, alder, pine, spruce, and oak (acorns). Insects are hard to find now, too, with most dead or hibernating. Provide the standard seed mix. This is the time when it is very important to include high-fat foods like peanut butter and suet. Fat is metabolized very efficiently into energy and will provide much more energy than a comparable amount of plant food. High energy fat foods are especially important for the insectivores since they are used to this kind of diet.

As winter ends and spring begins there is a temptation to stop feeding. The days are warm and maybe the migratory species are already gone. There should be enough natural food to support your local birds. Don't chance it. Continue feeding late into the spring. If you disband your flock by leaving the feeders empty, an early spring storm and cold snap can have devastating results on winter-weakened birds.

## Spring

As stressed above, it is very important to continue feeding your birds until you are absolutely certain there won't be an extended period of stormy, inclement, cold weather that will make it impossible for them to find sufficient food. I like to wait a little longer, too, when I don't feed all year, until I am sure that the natural foods birds rely on are available. Another bonus of spring feeding is that by maintaining a good food supply all spring you will encourage many birds to stay and nest in your area who otherwise might have gone elsewhere.

## Summer

For most birds, summer is a time of plenty. Natural foods are available, their food requirements are not so critical due to the friendlier weather, and exposure to the elements does not take such a toll. For birds raising a family of nestlings, however, finding enough food for themselves and the hungry little ones is a hardship that can be lessened if there is a well-stocked feeder nearby. In addition, summer is the time to be sure water is available. Scientists have noted that in many areas the only natural water source for birds is miles away. Other than these sources, the birds in the area must rely on puddles, sprinklers, birdbaths, and other man-supplied watering places.

The natural foods available at this time are fruits and berries, flower pods and seeds, grasses, and an abundance of insects. Feeders should be stocked with "light" foods, seed mix, as always, but also scraps, fruit, and bread. High energy foods like suet and peanut butter are not so critical as in winter but will still attract many insectivores.

Providing food during the summer will encourage more birds than ever to visit your yard and perhaps nest there. It will also build up a population of regular visitors who can be the nucleus of your winter flock.

Feeding through the year allows you to really get involved with the bird visitors around you. You learn to recognize individuals and family groups that visit. You watch courting and nesting, and often you get to observe as the parent birds raise their young and teach them to fly. You will find you get to observe a lot of bird behavior even if you work and are gone most of the day.

## INS AND OUTS OF FEEDING

There are many choices to be made when it comes to feeding birds—whether or not to use a feeder, which type of feeder, whether to feed on the ground, what seed mixes to try, whether to mix your own formula, etc. The main consideration, of course, should be what is good and convenient for *you*. A commercial mix packaged in handy, small quantities and an inexpensive tray feeder might be just right for the amount of time, money, and interest you have to spare. Others might prefer a more elaborate feeder or a combination of feeder and ground feeding. This section gives a broad overview of methods of providing food for the wild birds around you and some related subjects.

### Feeders

Although many people are happy to simply toss their bird food on the ground, most people have some type of specialized feeder. I recommend using feeders even if you are also ground feeding as different species of birds have different preferences and feeding styles. For example, ground birds like sparrows are very happy pecking up seed mix from the ground, but chickadees are very insecure about it. Providing for each feeding style is easy and will bring you a lot more birds. In addition, using a feeder keeps the food off the ground and, therefore, is cleaner.

Feeders come in almost every imaginable size, style, and color. Some are fixed on poles and some swing freely. Some are simple trays for seed; others are shaped like cute little Swiss chalets. I will give you my own preferences, along with designs and plans in Chapter 6 on feeders, but I will just look at the main considerations concerning the use of feeders.

General rules for using feeders are to choose them carefully, mount them securely, locate them in places as well protected from weather and enemies as possible, and, above all, keep them filled. Be aware that the birds are counting on your feeder. Also realize that the birds that come early might be eating all the feed, leaving little or none for the birds that come at other times during the day. I have had to put out additional feed in the early evening for a family of cardinals that insisted on coming at dusk each day after all the other feed was gone.

## Ground Feeding

Ground feeding is the easiest way to feed birds. You don't need any special feeders or any expense other than the feed mix itself, and there is minimal work involved. You simply spread the seed mix, scraps, or whatever other feed you choose out on the ground. There are, naturally, advantages and disadvantages.

Many species, especially doves and sparrows, are very comfortable on the ground and even prefer feeding there. Many other species are not at all willing to feed on the ground, however. Most of the real treetop-dwelling species will only reluctantly feed off the ground. In addition, spreading feed out on the ground can attract insects, squirrels, and even rats. Another problem is that if your feeding area is grass, some of the seeds will be lost in the roots and thatch, where it may or may not be hunted out by the birds. Birds are vulnerable to attack by cats and dogs while feeding on the ground, too. Experienced ground feeding birds are wary and watchful. In bad weather, feed thrown out for ground feeding can be covered by snow, making it useless. You can avoid this by spreading your feed out on a sheet of canvas, which can be picked up and shaken free of snow. In recent times, experts have speculated that feeding on the ground can cause the spread of disease among flocks of birds, both by causing them to crowd together while feeding and by contaminating the ground in that spot with spoiled feed and bird droppings. Other scientists have disputed this, citing examples in nature of small areas serving as gathering and feeding places of large numbers of birds without an increase in disease.

Despite all the possible disadvantages, there is a solid advantage to ground feeding that causes me to recommend it as a part of your feeding program. This advantage is that you can use ground feeding to attract and accommodate birds that might otherwise crowd your feeder and drive away more timid and desired individuals. A scoop thrown down under your main feeder or even off to one side of the yard will attract the sparrows, doves, cowbirds, and starlings that otherwise will overwhelm you. My practice is to keep a tray feeder filled for smaller or shy birds and then to throw down about a coffee can full for the insatiable appetites of the doves who line the power lines each morning waiting for me. I often have 30 to 40 fat doves in the yard, and they would really cause a problem if not for the fact that they are ground fed in a corner away from my #1 feeder.

## Competition

Whether you feed using a feeder or on the ground or a combination of both, you will see lots of competition among the birds you attract. Birds of different species will squabble and peck at each other, often driving one another off. The same thing happens with birds of the same species. A group of sparrows or cowbirds will be feeding peacefully until a newcomer arrives and proceeds to try and drive every other bird away from the feed. You will get to know the bullies in your flock of regulars very quickly.

One year in my flock of regular sparrow visitors the boss bird was, of all things, a bright yellow parakeet that had escaped from a neighbor up the street. We kept a close watch on him, never expecting him to make it through the first cold snap. As time went on, however, we were amazed to see him thrive in the cold outdoors and become a total bully to the other birds. The sparrows would usually begin arriving early in the morning, and by 9 A.M. there would be a noisy bunch feeding outside. You could always tell when the bully arrived, though, because of the chatter that would rise as he went around and around the feeder fighting, flapping his wings, and screeching until every other bird was driven off. It got so bad that even the doves would fly off when he landed on the feeder! The only birds that were not intimidated by him were the blue jays, but then they are masters of bullying, themselves. I spent many mornings fuming at that parakeet, but I missed him when he disappeared in the early spring.

I don't worry too much about the competition that goes on around the feeders in my yard. After all, it is totally natural. In every aspect of their live birds compete: for food, nesting sites, mates, etc. I do try to alleviate as much of the squabbles as possible, however, by maintaining two feeders to allow the birds to spread out more and by ground feeding. This way there is more room and less to fight about. Although most birds are at least somewhat territorial and many are *very* territorial, most will share a feeding area without too much trouble.

## Coping With Cats and Squirrels

Cats and squirrels are a problem at one time or another to nearly anyone who feeds wild birds. The squirrels are attracted by the feed you provide, and the cats lurk about hoping for a quick kill. I can give suggestions, but not solutions; I have not found one myself.

We feed the birds every year, all year. We also have two cats we love dearly. It sounds like a contradiction, and it is not a perfect situation, but it does work, and it makes me a little less militant about the cat problem. First of all, let me say that the birds who come to your yard will learn very quickly if there are cats living about and will be very cautious. Blue jays will turn out to be terrifically alert sentries, setting off an awful screeching whenever they spy a cat. They re especially valuable in this capacity because they spend a lot of time sitting high in nearby trees, which is an excellent position for keeping watch. When the blue jays set up their racket, the whole flock of feeding birds will take flight. Because they are used to watching for them, few birds will be lost to local cats. More are lost when birds used to a yard and vicinity with no regular cats are ambushed by strays who come hunting.

We have done a number of things to lessen the effects of the hunting efforts of our cats. Our feeders are placed high in trees; they are not near any branches from which a cat can leap or ambush. Our ground feeding area is out away from nearby cover plants and bushes that the cats can hide in. When we have used pole-mounted feeders in the past, we have mounted them on slick metal poles that cats and squirrels could not climb. Our cats have worn bells at times, too, to warn birds away. (This is something you might suggest to your neighbors if their cats are the problem.) All of these suggestions will help, but even the most careful precautions will not be 100 percent effective. The cats will get an occasional bird regardless. I accept this fact knowing that the number of birds lost to cat predation is still far less than the number of birds that would not make it through the winter without my feeding.

Squirrels can be a serious nuisance, too, around a feeder. I have seen them stuffed so full of choice sunflower seeds they could not fully close their mouths. They can really make a dent in your feed bill. It can be almost impossible to keep them off your feeders. They can jump 8 to 10 feet from a branch or roof onto the feeder. They can climb all but the slickest poles and cables. Squirrel and cat cones, as described in Chapter 6, will help but rarely totally prevent determined squirrels from reaching the food. I have heard some exotic solutions from harried bird lovers, such as fancy live trapping methods and even having them shot, but I prefer to take a more casual attitude. I do what I can to keep them away from the bird food, but if they manage to get to it, I figure they have to eat, too. On the positive side, they usually will not harm the birds at the feeder, and the birds often get so used to them that they don't even fly off at their arrival. Then, too, since cats usually frighten them off, you are not likely to have both problems at the same time. (This is an example of "looking on the bright side.")

# Chapter 3

# Foods For Birds

WHEN IT COMES TO SELECTING FOOD TO MAKE AVAILABLE to wild birds, you have it pretty easy. Wild bird food can be anything from table scraps to commercial seed mixes to elaborate homemade seed and suet mixes. With experience, you will learn what is convenient for you, within your budget, and favored by the bird population around you. It is always a good idea to try and maintain as balanced a diet as possible and to simulate the natural foods that are available as nearly as you can. Within those broad guidelines, the variety is nearly endless. In the following section, I will take a closer look at the main types of commonly used bird foods: commercial seed mixtures, kitchen scraps (suet, peanut butter, and other high-energy foods), custom seed mixtures, and suet and seed cakes. Then at the end, I have included a short section describing the basic diets of many common birds. A glance at it will help you decide which foods to offer.

## COMMERCIAL SEED FOODS

Commercial seed mixtures are the most common form of bird food used. They are readily available, packaged in almost any size you request, and moderately priced. In my local area, one feed store owner estimates that he sells more than a ton of commercial bird seed mixture each week in all sizes from 2-pound plastic bags to 50-pound grain sacks. Seed mixtures are also available in supermarkets, variety stores, and discount stores. They are mostly in small, convenient plastic sacks.

These commercial mixes have several strong advantages. The main advantage is the variety of packaging. Although I buy a variety of different seeds and other foods in bulk amounts and mix it myself, I occasionally buy a 50-pound sack of wild bird chow or game bird mixture. It is convenient for me to transport and store large amounts like this, but it isn't for others. These people can buy feed in smaller amounts. The common sizes are 2-, 3-, 5-, 10-, and 25-pound sacks. These smaller amounts can be stored right in the sack, unless rats and mice are a problem. I recommend storing the larger amounts in metal or plastic trash cans. These come in all sizes and usually are available with good, tight-fitting lids. I keep 50 to 75 pounds of bird food available for use on my back porch in a metal trash can. It is fully protected from weather and mice, and at the same time very easily portioned out in 3-pound coffee cans.

There are disadvantages to the commercial mixes. The first one is cost. While the commercial mixes are cheaper at feed stores than at discount stores or supermarkets, they are still more expensive than custom mixes you make up yourself. Of course, it may be worth the extra expense to you *not* to have to mix feed yourself. Also, the larger sizes, 25 and especially 50-pound sacks, are much cheaper by the pound than small sacks. Again, you might want to pay more for the convenience of smaller, portable packaging.

My main objection to commercial mixes is that unless you buy a reputable, name brand mix, you are liable to end up with a mix containing various "filler" seeds that might not be relished or eaten by your birds. Often you find weed seed, oat hulls, chaff, and all sorts of other matter in these bargain mixes as filler. You have to be very careful if you want to get your money's worth with many of the brands on the market.

Even the reputable, brand name mixes might not be exactly what you need for your bird population. These mixes are often formulated for game birds or certain species and contain seeds that your local birds might not prefer. Also, it is common for manufacturers to vary their seed mixture to include whatever seeds are cheap at the time. I don't find these factors to be a serious enough problem to warrant passing the seeds up. Usually it is only one component out of the entire mix that is not a favorite, and it turns out that, while they might leave it until last, it gets eaten, too.

When shopping for a commercial seed mixture, read the ingredient label carefully. Most mixes contain millet, milo, oats, wheat, and sunflower seeds. These are proven favorite foods that are sure to be eaten and enjoyed by your birds. Be careful about mixes that contain large proportions of other seeds. Be sure that they are seeds that will be eaten by the majority of your local birds. Here again, what you want to avoid is spending money for filler seeds instead of high-quality food.

## KITCHEN FOODS FOR BIRDS

Most of us, at one time in our lives or another, have fed bread scraps to the birds outside. This is a favorite activity for children. You will find that nearly all types of scraps from the kitchen are welcomed by the birds outside in your yard. Scraps provide variety in their diet, and experts speculate that it is the extra salt in some of these foods that makes them especially attractive. I would not say I would recommend scraps as the total diet, but they are a good addition. I personally would rather feed them to the birds than throw them out. The only caution I will offer is that if you put the scraps on the ground near your house, you will probably attract more insects and mice than you will with seed mix or suet.

Of all the scraps, bread foods are most commonly fed. Any type of bread food will do: white, wheat, biscuits, cornbread, etc. You will find that cardinals, juncoes, red-winged blackbirds, grackles, jays, robins, sparrows, and wrens especially look forward to scraps of bread. It is not a particularly nutritious food, but it is cheap and very much loved. It is also a very good food to use to initially attract birds because it is usually white and very easy for birds to spot on the ground or in a feeder. Often it takes weeks for birds to find a new feeder simply because they could not see any food near it. Seeds, being colored as they are, are hard to see from a distance; bread scraps are light colored, and there is a tendency to leave them in larger pieces. I have had very good luck establishing feeders when I have put bread scraps out first.

Fruits and nuts are especially good kitchen foods to provide. Until they become so expensive, raisins and peanuts were favorite foods of many of my regular visitors. These foods would be gone within minutes of my filling the feeder. Apples, sliced or chunked, are very popular foods, and they keep well on the feeder. With these larger fruits it is always a good idea to cut them into pieces small enough for birds to handle. Smaller pieces also mean that larger birds cannot fly off with the whole chunk. Birds also like oranges, chopped into may small pieces, as well as peaches, plums, and grapes.

26

You will be surprised to see which kitchen foods are preferred by the birds outside your home. I was amazed at first to see how much the mockingbirds around my yard loved meat scraps. In fact, one morning I looked out on my patio to find one pecking bits of barbecued spareribs left on our grill from the night before. I generally put out cheese, rice, leftover potatoes, macaroni and other noodles, sometimes oatmeal, beans, and just about anything from the table. If it is a new food, I watch carefully, and if it has not been eaten in a few hours, I take it away to keep spoiled food from building up in the feeder. If you have a good colony of birds established, some of them should find your "experimental" food within a couple of hours. If none begin to eat it, it is a good sign that you should remove it.

Another kitchen food that makes a good addition to birds' diets is dry dog food. Most of these foods are made from vegetable products like corn and wheat. Regular bird foods have ingredients added to boost the amount of protein up to at least 7 percent. I prefer to use dog food because it is much cheaper than dry cat food. It is easy to crush to the right size in a blender or by placing some in a plastic bag and running a rolling pin over it.

As you can figure, scrap feeding does not lend itself well to just any type of feeder. Many designs cannot handle bulkier foods like bread or other scraps. Tray feeders are great. They will handle any types of scraps you care to provide while keeping them up off the ground and away from ground insects, rats, mice, cats, dogs, and children.

## SUET AND PEANUT BUTTER

When winter really sets in and both the days and nights are cold, birds' energy needs skyrocket. Not only is the overall energy requirement for survival raised, but their main sources of food become scarce. At this time of year, seeds and other vegetable foods are extremely important. This is the time for foods that are really efficient, ones that can be metabolized into concentrated sources of energy. Fats are needed. When fats are metabolized they provide a much higher proportion of high-quality energy than a comparable amount of vegetable matter. The way to allow for this very important component of the winter diet is to provide suet, peanut butter, or some other form of fat in your feeders.

The cheapest, easiest source of fat to provide is suet. It is easy to acquire, needs no refrigeration, and can be served in a variety of ways. I consider it the best substitute for insects and larvae and an outstanding source of winter energy.

You will find that serving suet will bring a whole new group of birds to your feeder. There are some birds who are so nearly total insectivores that they will not readily eat seeds. These are the ones you will attract with suet as their regular diet of insects becomes scarce. Flickers, woodpeckers, jays, chickadees, starlings, titmice, thrashers, robins, thrushes, kinglets, wrens, mockingbirds, catbirds, orioles, juncoes, and sparrows love suet and will often become regular visitors to suet stations.

My local butcher sells me suet for 10 cents a pound. If I ask him to run it through his meat grinder, he charges 15 cents. It is a great bargain because that pound usually lasts from a week to two weeks. I had to look around a bit, though, to find this steady source. Many large chain supermarkets now receive their meat cut into sections instead of in sides or whole animals. This makes it a little more difficult to find suet in these markets. It is not that they don't want to help. When the meat is cut into sections at the packing plant, most of the suet is removed and used for other products. The market just does not receive much of it. I have found in my local area that if I am willing to wait a few days, the meat cutters will save scraps they trim from roasts and steaks until they get an amount large enough for me. Since I am in the store every few days anyway, this is no inconvenience.

Suet can be put out exactly as it comes from the meat market on a tray feeder or in the crotch of a tree. The problem here, however, is that if the pieces are anywhere small enough to allow a bird to carry off the whole chunk, that is what he will do. Jays, grackles, mockers, and even little sparrows will do their best to make off with the whole bundle. To avoid this, I suggest using a suet cage of some type. This can be as simple as a piece of curved, 1/2-inch-hardware cloth wired to a tree trunk and bent closed at the bottom as shown in Fig. 3-1. The 1/2-inch mesh is plenty large enough to allow the birds to peck off chunks of suet, but it won't allow them to make off with all of it. Many feeder designs incorporate a suet feeder into their basic features. This will be discussed in Chapter 6.

Another simple and very functional way to serve suet is in mesh bags, such as those that potatoes or onions come in. Just be sure the mesh is not too small. My favorite suet bags have been made from the durable, strong plastic mesh bags that turkeys come in. The mesh is the right size, and it will last for months and months.

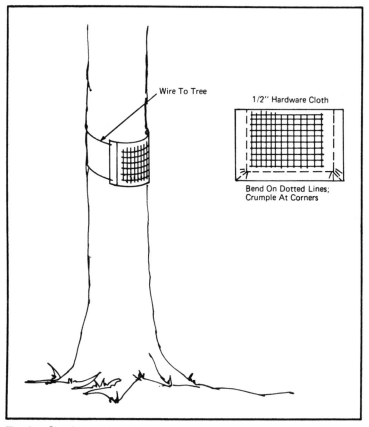

Wire To Tree

1/2" Hardware Cloth

Bend On Dotted Lines;
Crumple At Corners

Fig. 3-1. Simple bent hardware-cloth suet cage.

If you use a bag, all you have to do is hang it from a nail on your feeder or attach it to a tree branch or trunk.

I mentioned above that I usually ask my butcher to run the suet I buy through his meat grinder. I do this for two reasons. First of all, after he grinds the suet at the coarsest setting, it is just right to place in suet bags and be a lot easier for the birds to peck at than whole chunks. You would be surprised at how much work it is for small birds to peck off a piece of cold, firm suet from a large chunk in a suet rack or bag. It is much easier for them if it is coarsely ground. They can peck off a chunk and fly off with it. It also lessens the chance of a large bird coming along and managing to steal the whole chunk. The second reason for having the suet ground is that if you plan to serve it in a log feeder or suet cup, it will have to be melted first, and it is a real chore to try and evenly melt chunk suet. Chapter 6 contains a project for building a log feeder.

A couple of cautions about serving suet. First, suet will slowly melt, even in winter, and streak down whatever it is attached to. Tree trunks and branches will acquire a dark, greasy stain. For this reason, never attach a suet bag or feeder to your house or garage. The stains are definitely unsightly. Also, you will find that cats love suet and will steal it if given a chance. I have seen our own tom deftly climb the tree trunk up to where I had wired on a suet bag, cling there by three paws, neatly slice open the plastic mesh, and take off carrying the suet with a smug look on his face. Be sure to locate the suet feeder with the same rules in mind that you use for locating your seed feeder.

Over the years, people have told me and I have read about using bacon grease and other kitchen fats such as lard as a substitute for suet in the winter. I have tried using bacon grease several winters with always the same result; that is, it is not eaten until there is absolutely nothing else. I have tried smearing it on tree branches, mixing it with seed mix, and serving it from a suet cup. My local birds do not like it. This is an example of what I mean when I repeat over and over that you have to try various foods with your local birds. It is likely that in a different part of the country with a different set of birds and species, bacon grease would be a good winter food. Give it a try. It will certainly be a cheap source of fat for winter energy.

When I was a youngster and first began feeding birds, one of my favorite winter foods was peanut butter. It was cheap, easy to store and use, and many of my favorite species of songbirds loved it. At school we had projects where we took large pinecones and rolled them in peanut butter, filling all the cracks and spaces. Then we rolled them in seed mix and hung them out for the birds. You might remember doing the same sort of thing. As I recall, it took about a third of a jar of peanut butter for each large pinecone. That was when peanut butter was one of the cheapest foods on the supermarket shelf, though. Recently, when I thought about doing the same project for my second grade class, I quickly learned that peanut butter isn't cheap anymore.

Even though too expensive for most of us to use as a regular feeder food, peanut butter is a favorite of many birds, and it is another valuable, high-fat winter food. Creepers, chickadees, and nuthatches especially love it, as do most of the other insectivores. I have heard that some people receive out-of-date bulk peanut butter from nearby producers for use as bird food. If you have this opportunity, take advantage of it; your birds will love it.

As to serving peanut butter, the easiest ways are the best. Smear it on rough tree bark, serve it on pinecone feeders, or place it in suet cups secured to your feeders, tree branches, or tree trunks. You can also serve it in log feeders as described in Chapter 6.

Just as cats love suet, you will find that squirrels love peanut butter. I have found that they become more determined to reach peanut butter than they ever are to reach seeds. If they become a serious problem, you might try switching over to suet for a while. This is not their favorite food, and after a time, they generally get discouraged and move on. Then you can switch back to peanut butter.

## CUSTOM SEED MIXES

As you get more and more involved in bird feeding, you will probably consider mixing your own special seed mixture from bulk ingredients. I heartily recommend this because it is the one real way to arrive at a bird diet that is perfect for you, your locale, and the bird population around you. Feeding your own custom mix means you won't have the waste so common when you feed a commercial mix of various seeds. Once you have done a little experimenting to see which seeds are favorites, you will have no waste at all. You will also be able to supply in your mixes ingredients aimed at attracting certain species or feeding other species cheaper than with commercial mixes. For example, cracked corn is cheaper by far than commercial mix, and doves love it. If you have many doves to feed, it is much cheaper to mix in some cracked corn than to feed them their fill of commercial mix. You will find many instances like this where you can customize the diet of the birds in your yard by using a homemade seed mixture.

Unless you are from a farm background, when you walk into your local feed store and ask for seeds for wild birds, you will probably be amazed at the variety of different foods available. Most stores carry *millet* (parakeet seed), sunflower seeds, oats, wheat, milo, barley seed, and cracked corn. Feed store owners who cater to a large number of people who like to mix bird foods generally carry hemp seed, buckwheat, rape seed, and other seeds, too. A little experimenting will teach you which ones you should include in your mix. Just buy a pound or so of each variety you are considering and try them out in an established tray feeder. (Most of these seeds sell for between 15 and 35 cents a pound.) The easiest way I have found for this experiment is to tack a divided aluminum "TV dinner" tray onto the feeder and place a different type of seed in each compartment. Keep track of which type of seed is always left until last (or not eaten at all), and you will get a picture of the preferred foods of the birds around you. Concentrating on these seeds will get you a mix that will attract a large number of birds and not be wasted.

Of course, another consideration in deciding on which seeds to include in a mixture is cost. While nearly any homemade mixture will be cheaper than a commercial mix, the actual costs of different homemade mixtures varies greatly. When you begin to figure which seeds to include and the cost of the mix, you will have to make judgment calls in deciding whether to include a relatively expensive seed that the birds loved or a less expensive one that was popular. Be a careful shopper. A type of seed that sounds cheap by the pound might not be if a large proportion of its weight is not actually edible seed but hull or shell instead. It generally helps to look at the seed and try to get an idea of the relative number of seeds per pound and the number of birds a pound of each of the various seeds might feed. This will help you get your money's worth.

In a recent government study on wild bird feeding, naturalists discovered that regardless of the varied seeds offered in the feeders, the two overwhelming favorites all over the country were white proso millet (commonly available as parakeet seed) and oil-type sunflower seeds. When I read that fact, I was really pleased because over the years I have come to the same conclusion. Everywhere I have lived I have had wonderful luck with these two seeds. Birds everywhere from California to South Dakota to Florida have preferred them. In addition, I rely on them because they're always available locally and are about the cheapest of all the seeds. Any seed eater will eat millet. Sunflower seeds are loved especially by cardinals, finches, nuthatches, crossbills, chickadees, grackles, and jays. If you have the room, sunflowers can be grown in the home garden and either harvested when ripe or left there for the birds to peck at naturally. I suggest that for overall success, any mixture you make up should start with these two seeds as a base. From there, any favored seeds that will maintain a balanced diet may be added.

As your bird population grows, you may want to modify your custom seed mix to include other specialized foods. The most common addition is "scratch" feed. Scratch feed usually consists of cracked corn, milo, and wheat. It is sold as chicken feed in 25- and

50-pound sacks or in bulk amounts. The advantage of adding scratch feed is that it is a nutritious, cheap extender. Many species of birds will eat it, and the corn is especially preferred by grackles, doves and other game birds, jays, and sparrows. Scratch feed offers a cheaper way to "fill up" the doves and other big eaters that are bound to gather around your feeders. Another addition that is nutritious and inexpensive is baby chick feed. This comes in bulk amounts or in 25- and 50-pound sacks, and it is eaten by many species of birds. It is high in carbohydrates and vitamin A.

After you have done your basic experimenting to see which seeds are favored by your local birds, and after you have considered cost and made a decision as to the ingredients in your custom seed mix, it is time to actually buy and mix it. I suggest calling around to a few feed stores to shop for the best price. you will be surprised at the variation in prices of the same seed. Generally, I have found that stores that cater to urban and suburban shoppers, bird feeders, and "horsey" people charge higher prices than feed stores operated mainly for a farm clientele. If you have the opportunity to save by buying at a farm store, take advantage of it. Not only will you save money, but you will probably find seeds and advice on mixes that are unavailable elsewhere.

When you go to purchase the bulk seed and other ingredients for your mix, unless you buy it in stock 25- or 50-pound sacks, it will probably be stored in bins or sacks. Take a look at it. You are looking for evidence of mold or large amounts of stems, weeds, and other waste materials. The seed or feed should be perfectly dry and free running when you run your hand through it. The scent should be a pleasant, grass-like one, never moldy. If you are unsure of the quality of the seed you are looking at, don't buy it. A small amount of mold in an ingredient can spread and ruin a whole batch of bird food.

After your trip to the feed store, you will end up with your ingredients in a group of plastic or paper sacks. My suggestion is to buy a large trash can to mix and store it in. I have a standard, galvanized 33-gallon can that will hold about 100 pounds of bird seed mix or about a month's worth for my birds. A tight-fitting lid is important to keep moisture out of the seed. It also serves to keep out rats and mice. Two cats, rats, and mice have not been a problem for me, but they could easily be one for you if you try to keep seed in paper or plastic sacks in the garage. A trash can also has a large mouth to allow for easily pouring in the ingredients (when you are trying to pour in 25 or 50 pounds this is important) and to allow you to easily reach in to fill your scoop with bird food down to the last few pounds in the bottom. It is much easier to handle than a bulky plastic sack or a cardboard box that gets bent sides and dented corners. The handles make it portable, too.

If you are adding new custom mix to bird food already in the can, I advise pouring out the older food into a plastic sack or something, mixing the new, and replacing the older food on top. This ensures that the older food is eaten first instead of being left to mold on the bottom of the can. Because you are likely to be mixing up a fairly large amount of feed, 25 pounds or more, I don't suggest pouring all of each ingredient into the can at a time. This makes it harder to completely mix each type of food with the others. I like to pour about one sixth of each type in until I have some of each, then I mix it well. When mixed, I add another one sixth of each and repeat. It does not take any extra time, and the mixture comes out pretty uniform.

Although I encourage you to experiment and come up with your own special custom seed mix based on the favorite foods of your local birds and the cost and availability of feed near you, I do have a basic custom mix that I have had good luck with in different parts of the country. It is a rather inexpensive mixture and for simplicity is based on commercially available wild bird food. Just let me stress that you should be careful to buy a good brand of wild bird food. The basic recipe is:

> 25-pound sack of wild bird food
> 15 pounds white proso millet
> 10 pounds sunflower seeds
> 10 pounds scratch feed

Mix up a batch and try it. Then alter the ingredients to suit your own birds.

## SUET SEED CAKES

One of the neatest and best ways to supply both suet and seed mixture to your birds is by making up batches of suet seed cakes. These are made of melted suet and any number of other ingredients from plain millet to bread crumbs to oats. Suet seed cakes are easy and fun to make, especially for children, and are very much liked by most birds.

There are many, many recipes for making suet seed cakes and

just about any one that the birds will eat is good. In deciding on your recipe, take into consideration the same things you did for your overall feeding diet. Try to maintain a balanced diet and try to include as ingredients foods that the birds in your local area like. You might have to do some experimenting with different ingredients to see which are eaten with gusto and which are eaten only when nothing else is available. The easiest way to do this is to provide a variety of foods at an established feeder, in separate containers, and note over a period of a few days the favorite foods and the ones that are not eaten. Then you will have a good idea of what to include in your recipe.

The major component of suet seed cakes is, naturally, suet. As you read in the section on suet and peanut butter, suet is cheap, easy to store and handle, a very important source of winter energy. It is also a favorite food substitute for insectivores. It can be served straight from the butcher, coarsely ground, or melted and molded into portions. For our purposes, I recommend that you have the butcher run your suet through his grinder. Mine does this service for me for very little charge, and it saves me doing it myself. If your suet is unground, you should go ahead and grind it in a food processor or grinder. The grinding helps by making the next step, melting, much easier.

If your suet has been ground, it should melt uniformly over medium-low heat. If not ground, it should be chopped as fine as possible, and then melted. For the smoothest suet that blends best into the other ingredients, allow it to cool and solidify completely, and then remelt it. I generally skip this step, because I prefer to have my suet cakes remain a little lumpy. It is a matter of preference. Try it both ways.

While you wait for the suet's second melting, decide on and assemble the molds you need and the other ingredients. Any kind of mold will do, depending on the size and shape of the finished cakes you want. I have used heavy aluminum foil shaped into rectangles, margarine tubs, even ice cube trays, and all worked fine. As for the other ingredients, you can use almost anything considered a bird food: bread crumbs, seeds, corn meal, raisins, crushed dog food, anything your birds like. Simply place these other ingredients in the molds up to about one-half or two-thirds of the way full and pour melted suet over them to the top of the mold. Allow the mixture to cool and harden. This can be hurried by placing the molds in the refrigerator or freezer. Then, when fully solidified, flex the mold to pop out the cakes or peel off the aluminum foil, and they are ready to serve from a feeder or in suet bags. If not needed right away, suet seed cakes will last for long periods of time without refrigeration or indefinitely in the freezer.

Over the years, I have tried many different suet seed cake recipes, mainly because I was using whatever I had on hand at the time. One of my luckiest accidents came about when I decided to try some turtle food left over from one of my children's pets. I knew it was a very high protein food, so it should appeal to insectivores and that was whom I was trying to attract. The turtle food suet seed cakes were a big hit on the feeder, and ever since, when I have had it, I have used a package of one kind or another of high protein fish or other animal food. So-called ant eggs (which are actually ant larvae), tubifex worms, dried shrimp, and anything the pet store sells has worked well except the products that are very fishy tasting. As I said, experiment until you optimize your own special recipe. Until then, if you want an easy recipe to start with, try my basic one.

1 cup course bread crumbs<br>
1 cup millet seed<br>
1 small package ant eggs or tubifex worms<br>
Enough melted suet to bind

Mix all the ingredients except for the suet, and place them in the bottom of the molds to the halfway mark. Fill the rest of the way with melted suet. Give each mold a quick stir to mix the ingredients and allow it to harden as mentioned above.

## GRIT

The last item to consider providing for the local birds is one many people don't think of—grit. Grit is an important part of birds' diets. They must have it to help grind the hard seeds and other foods they eat, much the same way our teeth act to break up our food. Grit can be supplied in feeders, in special cups attached to feeders, or in suet seed cakes. Some forms of grit that can be offered are: fine sand, crushed charcoal, or crushed eggshells. Eggshells have the small advantage of also supplying calcium in the diet. I certainly do not consider grit as important to provide as food, water, or shelter, but, after all, what we are trying to do is make things easier for the birds, isn't it?

## COMMON BIRD DIETS

One of the first things you will do when you decide to feed birds in your garden is take a mental survey of which birds you can reasonably expect to attract. You will use this survey to help decide which foods to provide on your feeders. If the birds you seek to attract are mostly insectivores, you will certainly want to provide suet as a regular food. Fruit eaters will be attracted more by apples, raisins, and grapes. You will consider which seeds to include in the mix you provide for the seed eaters. All of this implies a knowledge of birds and their preferred diets. There are a great many books on the subject that I recommend you look over, but for starters, some brief thumbnail sketches of common birds' diets will help you.

Before beginning, let me say that birds' diets are not absolutely constant. The same type of birds' diet may vary greatly due to regional differences and availability of plant and animal foods. Diet also varies by season. Birds who might well prefer insects will surely turn to a seed diet when insects are scarce in winter. Bird species who visit feeders in one part of the country might not in another. Use the diet sketches only as a starting point, not as a hard-and-fast rule.

**Bluebirds.** Bluebird diets consist of between 65 percent and 80 percent animal matter and the rest vegetable. They enjoy wild cherries, dogwoods, wild grapes, cedar berries, mulberries, blueberries, elderberries, serviceberries (also called juneberries), and holly berries. Use fruits to attract them.

**Buntings.** Buntings are mostly seed eaters but will take a few insects. Try a good seed mix with some fruits and nuts to bring them to the feeder.

**Cardinals.** These bright birds are friendly regulars at feeders. They prefer to feed early in the morning or late in the afternoon. They especially love sunflower seeds as well as seed mix, blackberries, blueberries, wild cherries, dogwood, wild grapes, elderberries, and tulip tree fruit.

**Catbirds.** Catbird diets are pretty evenly divided between animal and vegetable foods. They enjoy blackberries, wild cherries, dogwoods, wild grapes, cedar berries, mulberries, Virginia creeper, elderberries, serviceberries, holly berries, bayberries, and buckthorn. Although sometimes aggressive enough to drive away more timid birds, catbirds will frequent feeders in search of seed mix, fruits, and occasionally kitchen scraps.

**Cedar Waxwings.** Waxwings are often seen traveling in large flocks, and you will get a treat if a whole group stops by your yard. The best way to attract them is to have the natural foods they eat growing there because they are somewhat shy about feeders. Their main diet is blackberries, wild cherries, dogwoods, wild grapes, cedarberries, mulberries, spruce berries, black gum fruit, elderberries, serviceberries, holly berries, hawthorn fruit, buffalo berries, and persimmons.

**Chickadees.** Chickadees are overwhelmingly animal food eaters by about 80 percent to 20 percent vegetable. Still, you can attract them to feeders, especially if there is suet or peanut butter available. Include seed mix, too, with sunflower seeds and dried fruits. In nature their foods include: pine seeds, acorns, maple seeds, birch seeds, elm seed, hemlock seed, fir seed, and bayberries.

**Creepers.** You will hear and see creepers in the trees around you but only rarely on a seed feeder. Creepers are insectivores and only eat a very small amount of vegetable matter. They do like suet and peanut butter, though, and will take it if offered on tree branches or trunks near their natural food finding areas.

**Crows.** Crows are often bold enough to visit suburban feeders. They usually will come in small groups of two to four birds. Their diet consists of about 80 percent vegetable matter and cracked corn is a favorite.

**Doves.** Like the other game birds, doves' main diet is seeds and grain, although they will take a few insects. If you live in their normal range, seed mix and especially cracked corn will soon attract all the doves you care to have at your feeder.

**Finches.** While they will eat a few insects, finches' diet is nearly 100 percent seeds and other vegetable matter. At the feeder any good seed mix with sunflowers will draw them. Their natural foods include: dogwood fruit, cedarberries, maple seeds, black gum fruit, elm seeds, tulip tree fruit, ash seed, aspen seed, and sweet gum seed.

**Flickers.** Flickers are mostly insectivores but will visit a feeder readily, especially for suet. My local birds also pick the sunflower seeds out of the seed mix.

**Goldfinches.** Goldfinches will take seed mixes from feeders and fruit as well. Their natural foods include: maple seed, elm seed, alder seed, and sweet gum seed.

**Grackles.** Once you have your feeder established, if there are any grackles in the area, they will be regular, noisy visitors. They enjoy seed mixes, fruits, suet, sunflower seeds, kitchen scraps, corn, and grain.

**Jays.** Jays are regulars to any nearby feeders. Their diet is about three-quarters vegetable matter and very varied. They will take seed mix, sunflower seed, acorns, fruits, kitchen scraps, and suet or peanut butter from the feeder. Other foods include: pine seeds, blackberries, cedarberries, blueberries, elderberries, beech seeds, hickory nuts, and bayberries.

**Juncoes.** Juncoes are common feeder visitors where any good seed mix will attract them. Other natural foods include pine seeds and sweet gum fruits.

**Kinglets.** Kinglets are nearly 100 percent insectivores, but they will visit seed feeders in winter. They will also become regular visitors to suet feeders.

**Mockingbirds.** Mockingbirds are another common visitor to feeders. Seed mixes are not favored, however. They prefer suet, kitchen scraps, sunflower seeds, and fruits. Natural foods include: blackberries, dogwood fruit, wild grapes, cedarberries, mulberries, Virginia creeper, black gum fruit, elderberries, serviceberries, greenbrier, holly berries, hackberries, and persimmons.

**Nuthatches.** These squeaky little birds frequent high treetops but will come to a feeder if they feel it is safe. They enjoy many different types of seeds as well as suet and peanut butter. Main natural foods are: pine seed, acorns, maple seed, spruce berries, Virginia creeper, elderberries, beech seeds, hickory nuts, and fir seeds.

**Orioles.** Orioles are mainly insectivores. They only eat an estimated 25 percent worth of vegetable matter. They can be fed fruits from a feeder as well as blackberries, mulberries, blueberries, elderberries, and serviceberries.

**Quail.** Being game birds, quail are attracted to seed mixes and to grains. If you have quail around you, a scoop or two or scratch feed or cracked corn will turn them into constant visitors. In nature their diets are about 40 percent animal matter and 60 percent vegetable, including acorns, pine seed, cedarberries, sumac seed, hackberries, Russian olive, wild roses, and mesquite.

**Robins.** Robins' diets are about evenly divided between animal and vegetable foods. At a feeder they will take suet, fruits, and kitchen scraps before seed mixes. Other natural foods include: blackberries, wild cherries, dogwood fruit, cedarberries, blueberries, serviceberries, holly berries, hackberries, persimmons, and buckthorns.

**Sparrows.** Sparrows' diets consist of about one-third animal foods and the rest vegetable. In nature, their main foods include: blackberries, wild cherries, dogwood fruit, Virginia creeper, elderberries, blueberries, hawthorn fruit, and hackberries. At a feeder they enjoy any seed mix, kitchen scraps, suet, fruits and nuts, and sunflower seeds and soon become constant visitors.

**Tanagers.** These lovely birds are fruit lovers and can be attracted to a feeder with apples, berries, oranges, grapes, and raisins. Some of their natural foods are: blackberries, wild cherries, dogwood fruits, mulberries, blueberries, black gum fruit, elderberries, serviceberries, and bayberries.

**Thrashers.** If you live on the edge of the woods, you will see thrashers. Their diet is about 40 percent animal and the rest vegetable. They enjoy pine seeds, blackberries, wild cherries, wild grapes, Virginia creeper, sumac, blueberries, elderberries, serviceberries, holly berries, buckthorn, and hackberries.

**Thrushes.** Great singers, thrushes are birds to try to attract to your yard. In winter, they will take suet, seed mix, and fruits from feeders. Natural foods include: blackberries, wild cherry, dogwood fruit, cedarberries, blueberries, elderberries, serviceberries, greenbrier, holly berries, and hackberries.

**Titmice.** Titmice are mainly insectivores, but, especially in the winter, they become regular visitors to feeders where they especially enjoy sunflower seeds, fruits, and suet, as well as seed mixes. Some of their natural foods are: pine seeds, acorns, blackberries, wild grapes, Virginia creeper, and beech seed.

**Towhees.** Towhees, while preferring an 80 percent insect diet, often become visitors at feeders near their nesting or wintering grounds. They are mainly woods birds with natural foods including: pine seed, blackberries, wild cherries, acorns, blueberries, elderberries, serviceberries, holly berries, aspen seeds, and sweet gum fruit. Offer them fruits, berries, suet, and seed mix, including sunflower seeds.

**Warblers.** Warblers can be coaxed to feeders in summer by offering fruits, raisins, and berries. In winter, they often will take seed mix and sunflower seeds as well as bread. Natural foods include fruits and berries of all kinds as well as pine seeds and holly berries.

**Woodpeckers.** While woodpeckers maintain a 75 percent to 25 percent balance of animal food to vegetable food, they often visit feeders in search of special favorite foods and suet. Some natural foods are: pine seeds, blackberries, wild cherries, acorns, mulberries, sumac, elderberries, blueberries, greenbrier, holly berries, hawthorn fruit, aspen seeds, palmettos, and hackberries.

**Wrens.** While their diets consist nearly 100 percent of animal foods, wrens will visit feeders when they nest or winter nearby. Offer fruits and seed mix, but suet will be a more popular choice.

# Chapter 4

# Shelter, Water, and Other Needs

P ROVIDING FEEDERS AND A GOOD, STEADY SUPPLY OF BIRD foods will attract many birds to your yard, but if you are to have the maximum number and if you want them to stay to winter or nest near you, you must also provide for their other needs. This is not to minimize the importance of feeding birds but rather to point out some often overlooked needs that are easy and fun to tend to and pay off in terms of numbers of birds you will count as regular visitors.

## SHELTER

Shelter for wild birds is just about anything. It can mean dense trees, comfortable birdhouses, the underside of a highway bridge, or simply the lee side of a building. If you watch them out on a cold, wet morning, you have surely wondered where they find shelter. If you have wondered about it, you have probably given some thought to how you could help. The answer is fairly simple because there are many different forms of shelter.

### Winter Shelter

The most basic forms of shelter are those designed to provide places for birds to escape from the worst of the winter weather. As I have stated before, winter survival is the biggest foe birds face.

Even with their remarkable physiological defenses against freezing, including the ability to slow down their body functions and lower their energy needs, exposure to the elements takes a terrible toll on birds each year.

In nature, birds find shelter among the densest trees around them. Pines, cedars, and all of the evergreens serve as windbreaks and shelters for birds. They often forget their territorial squabbles and peacefully share shelter in bad weather. If you have dense evergreens around you, they will be well used. If you don't, you might consider planting some of the faster growing varieties. Most are ornamental and will begin to serve as good shelter within a very short time.

Thick bushes are also very good shelter if they keep their foliage. Many of the bird species that prefer to roost and nest at lower heights will be very comfortable in a low bush. Many hedges shelter small flocks of birds all winter. Chapter 5 will list some bushes and trees that provide good shelter for birds.

If the winters are severe in your part of the country, you might want to consider building and putting up a bird box or two. This is a wooden box, often an altered packing crate, usually about 1 foot or 18 inches wide, 2 to 3 feet tall, and 1 foot or so deep. It is hung from the lee side of a building or a tree. Inside are perches extending out from the inside wall and staggered so that the birds do not roost directly over one another. As shown in Fig. 4-1, the opening to the box is near or at the bottom to minimize the loss of inside heat.

If you have placed the bird box in a secure, safe place and given the birds time to get familiar with it early in the fall and winter, you will probably have birds using the box all season. Sometimes boxes are absolutely overcrowded with tenants on severe nights. You will usually have a regular crew of box visitors and a varying number of transients who spend a night or two and then disappear. While they might squabble on the feeder, most of the time birds are completely peaceful in the box. Only once in a while have I seen aggressive birds drive away others who attempted to enter.

Another easily provided form of shelter is a simple, two- or three-sided shelf, like a robin shelf with an overhanging roof, positioned so that it provides protection from the wind and rain or snow. Shelves like this are also good if built without roofs, as windbreaks only, and placed so that the sun hits them in the winter. Then they become warm, wind protected gathering places for birds.

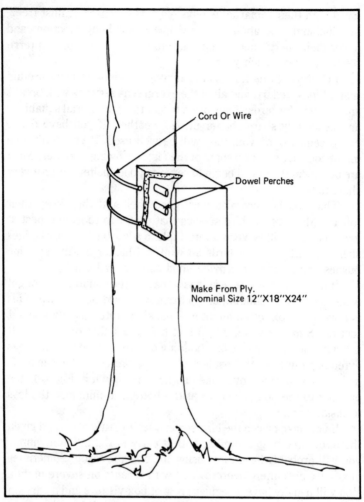

Fig. 4-1. Bird box for winter shelter.

## Birdhouses

The most common form of manmade shelter provided for birds is birdhouses. Putting up birdhouses is a very old pastime. Southeastern Indians practiced it hundreds, if not thousands, of years ago. After realizing the benefits of having purple martins around to rid the area of insects, the Indians began hanging birdhouses made from gourds on tall poles throughout their villages. There are numerous illustrations of this early practice, and the settlers who adopted the practice from the Indians passed it on to their descendants. Even today in rural areas of the south and midwest, you will see clusters of gourd houses hung high for purple martins to use.

Birdhouses are generally put up to accommodate nesting birds rather than simply as shelter. Many people leave their houses up and open all year, however. The houses are very popular during the winter, not only with sparrows and other birds, but squirrels like a warm place, too, and they will take over a house if they can. If the houses are used during the winter, it is especially important to give them a thorough cleaning before the nesting season.

Whether you leave your houses open as winter shelter or not, if they are to offer shelter and nesting places to the variety of birds you mean for them to, you must design, build, and place them correctly. In Chapter 7, which is devoted to birdhouse projects, there is a discussion of the kind of construction to use. There is also a chart with size, shape, and height requirements for many types of birds. Give it your attention, because it is the result of years of study by government naturalists. The simple fact that the size, shape, size of opening, etc., are critical for each type of bird. Many just won't use a house of the wrong specifications. A little research ahead of time will give you good results.

## PROVIDING WATER

A naturalist studying the effects of manmade feeders on songbirds in an eastern suburban area found that on the average the birds in his study were having to fly more than a half mile from their feeding and nesting areas to find water. That is quite a distance, and it serves to point out the importance of providing for another of birds' needs—water.

Water is easy to provide and sure to attract more birds to your yard. I have often had birds as regular visitors who did not visit the feeders or nest in the houses at all. They came every day for a dip in the water. Many times there would be two wholly separate groups of birds in the yard, those who were regulars and lived in or near my yard and those who flew in for water each day. Then, too, a readily visible source of water can attract passing or migrating individuals or sometimes whole flocks. A large group of 15 to 20 migrating birds can have trouble finding water in a strange area. If your water source is out in the open and easily spotted from the air, it can be very attractive.

It is most important to provide water in the summer when the weather is hot and many of the birds' common watering places like puddles and ponds begin to dry up. It is also a good idea to offer some water throughout the year, however. Even in the winter, a small amount of water kept thawed will be used and appreciated, and it will save the birds a longer trip through possibly bad weather.

There are many different types of containers you can use to provide water. No matter which one you finally decide on, a few general rules apply. First of all, place your water source out in the open where birds using it have a good view of approaching enemies. Do not place it near bushes or other cover that cats can ambush from. The water should be placed fairly near taller bushes or trees, however, so that birds can land there first to survey the area or flit there to escape enemies. The container should be shallow, from 1 to 3 inches deep. This will allow the birds to bathe and splash about in it. It is difficult for a bird to perch on the rim of a container and reach very far down inside to drink. Birds are generally happier with their water out in the sun, but in the summer this might cause the water to get too hot. You will have to either place it in partial shade or arrange for cooling it as described later.

### Raised Birdbaths

The best overall source of water you can provide is a raised birdbath, which makes it more difficult for cats to ambush drinking birds. Also, birds tend to feel much safer on them as they can see approaching enemies more easily, and they have a better chance of flying off to nearby cover. There are many types available in different styles and of different materials.

One of the most common types of raised baths is the cast concrete type. These are available at ornamental concrete works or often at gardening or landscaping shops. Their prices are usually reasonable considering the advantages over similar ones of plastic. Concrete baths last indefinitely and usually only break if they are dropped. They are rather heavy, which is very good, because it makes them stable and hard to tip over. They are easy to clean by swishing a brush around the bowl and then praying it out with a stream of water from a hose. The depth of these birdbaths is usually just right. If you shop around, you will end up with a bath that not only will fill the bill for many years but also look good in the yard, too.

Ceramic birdbaths have become popular in some parts of the country lately. There is even more variety in this type than in the concrete ones. In general, they have the same features, advantages, and disadvantages as concrete, except that they tend to be more expensive (although often also more attractive), and they tend to break under less impact.

Lately there have been many different models of high impact plastic birdbaths marketed. Some of these are very good and some are very bad. In general, plastic baths are inexpensive and often come designed so that you can detach the lightweight bowl part and remove it for cleaning. This is a good feature if it reattaches securely enough to prevent the bowl from tipping or wobbling. Many of the plastic ones are very light. This is nice, except that very light birdbaths are likely to tip over easily unless they are sunken into the ground or are equipped with a weighted pedestal base as many are. Another worry about plastic baths is that the lower grade plastics have a tendency to get brittle after a time out in the weather and crack. Plastic birdbaths come in a variety of attractive colors from traditional white to rustic brown and green. After a time in the sun, however, most of these colors fade out to an unattractive blotchiness. I do not mean to sound as though all plastic birdbaths are bad investments. This is far from correct. You simply should watch what you are buying and be careful to look for good features and materials as well as a good price.

Regardless of the type of materials used in construction, the raised birdbath should be shallow enough for birds to use comfortably and positioned out in the open but yet near cover. Designs for many different types of raised baths have been published in how-to-do-it books and magazines. The baths are made out of everything from sheet metal to poured concrete. If you are handy around the shop, you might want to build your own.

## Pools

Ornamental garden pools can be attractive additions to your landscaping as well as water sources for birds. They can be built simply in any shape or size out of mesh-reinforced concrete. In fact, I have seen prefabricated, high impact plastic garden pool kits complete with rocklike edging and a drainage system and pump. If you are willing to take up the yard space needed for this almost permanent installation and if you don't mind the upkeep involved, a garden pool might be just the thing for you.

If a pool is to be a source of water for the birds near you, be sure it meets the requirements. Design it so that it slopes gently at one end (at least). Be sure you have some means for cleaning the pool. I have seen many artfully-shaped, rock-edged pools left empty or full of rotten weeds because there was no easy, quick way to clean them. After all, a 100- or 200-gallon pool without a drainage system is tiring to bail, scrub, and refill.

While garden pools can be lovely landscaping additions, give them careful consideration before you build one. They *do* take up quite a bit of space, and they are virtually permanent if built into the ground with concrete. In addition, they are not the best form of birdbath because most are not shallow enough and are at ground level where birds are uncomfortable and in danger from ambushing cats.

## Other Waterers

If neither a raised birdbath nor a garden pool will fit your situation, you still have many ways to provide water for the birds. You are limited only by your creativity. In the past, I have used galvanized trash can lids and dishpans with brick islands set in them among other things. Any sort of container can be made to work. Trash can lids, whether metal or plastic, are shallow enough and stable when set in a slight depression of the ground. Plastic paint roller trays work very well because the built-in slope is just about right. Most of these suggestions are for ground level use although you can devise some means for placing them higher. I have even seen a cake pan fastened with angle brackets about 6 feet high on a tree trunk. There really are dozens of things that make quite satisfactory bird waterers.

## Keeping the Water Cool in the Summer

Since two of the suggested requirements of a good birdbath are that it be shallow and preferably out in the open where it is likely to be sunny, the water you provide for your birds is bound to get hot. I have gone out in the summer to refill my birdbath and found the water already very hot at 9:30 A.M. One obvious solution to the warm water problem is to change it frequently throughout the day in the summer. Few of us, however, even if we don't work during the day want to take the time to do it. Over the years, I have used two other solutions that are far better, the running hose line and the drip bucket.

If your birdbath is near enough to an outside water faucet, you might consider running a small hose out to it and letting a trickle

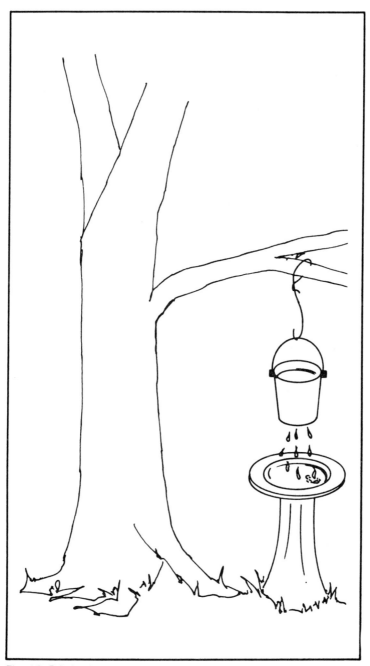

Fig. 4-2. Drip bucket method of keeping birdbath water cool.

of water run into it all day. Don't picture a fat, green garden hose draped over the side of your attractive birdbath; that isn't what I mean. You should plan a route from the faucet that will allow you to leave the hose and tubing in place when you mow the grass if possible. Then, attach a Y-connector to the faucet and a length of garden hose to it long enough to reach the base of your birdbath. The other side of the Y-connector should be capped off for you to use for regular sprinkling, etc. At the end of the garden hose near the base of your birdbath attach a reducer, available at any hardware store, of a size that will reduce the spout from garden hose size down to 1/4 inch or 3/8 inch. Attach that size tubing (also available at the hardware store) to the reducer and snake it up the side of your birdbath. Bed the tubing in place up the side and over the top in a good amount of silicone bathtub caulk. Use large rubber bands to hold it in place while it cures (about 24 hours). When cured and set, you can turn the water on to a mere trickle and have a stream running all the time to provide fresh, cool water.

My favorite means of keeping birdbath water cool is to use a drip bucket like the one shown on Fig. 4-2. To make one you take a 2 to 5 gallon bucket, punch a few holes in the bottom of it, and hang it from a convenient tree branch directly over your birdbath. Fill it up, and it will provide a steady drip of water into the bath to cool it and keep it filled at the same time. If you are careful and don't overdo the holes, the bucket will drip slowly enough to only need filling every few days. You will find that the birds love the splashing water, and it saves having to fool with a hose arrangement.

### Preventing Freezing

The opposite side of the coin from the summer hot water problem is the problem of having your birdbath freeze over in winter. It is a problem in the southeast where we get freezing temperatures several times a year, but it is much more serious in the north. There, often all sources of water for miles are frozen over, putting an extra hardship on wintering birds.

During the past few years, I have seen several new products come on the market in pet stores and specialty catalogs designed to solve this problem nicely. They range from plastic wafers through which heating wires run to heat sources designed and molded to look like stones. There are also good products available that were designed for farm use to keep water for livestock or poultry thawed. Most of these products are well designed and well constructed. Some of them, especially those built for farm use, are rather large and bulky but very reliable. Many found in pet shops are relatively more expensive than others that will do as well but not look so clever.

If you are unable to find a heater that suits you, an aquarium heater has done well for me for several winters. I recommend a 75-watt size, and an increase in the depth of the water to about 5 to 6 inches because most heaters' directions specify that they should be kept fully submerged. Use an all-weather extension cord to provide the electricity. Check the birdbath regularly to be sure the water level does not drop too much. Your water should stay thawed all winter even on the coldest nights.

## COVER

Cover is different from shelter. Instead of being intended to provide protection from the weather, cover is meant to provide secure resting places and protection from enemies. Nearby trees that birds use as safe temporary resting places or protection from enemies are cover. Secure cover also serves as nesting sites for many birds.

The most common cover is the natural kind—trees and bushes around the yard. You see birds using this kind of cover all the time as safe places to survey the area before they come closer. They also use cover as places to flit to in case they are disturbed or frightened by a potential enemy. Sometimes birds become so accustomed to having a set piece of cover that they are confused when it is cut down or moved. For example, one fall a group of titmice in my yard developed a pattern of flying to a small pecan tree first and waiting to be sure the cats were not around before coming to the feeder. There were other trees nearby that would have worked just as well, but they always used the pecan tree. This went on for nearly the entire winter until a February storm broke several of the branches and forced us to cut the little tree down. The next morning the titmice flitted into the yard as usual. They made right for the spot the tree had stood and, not finding it, circled around confused and agitated several times before flying off. It took several days for them to settle on another tree for their lookout.

If you have an older yard with established trees and bushes, you probably have enough cover to make the birds feel safe. Your main consideration will be to place houses and feeders so that the birds get full advantage of it. If, on the other hand, you are just getting your landscaping started or adding to a rather bare yard, you will want to add trees and plants that will give maximum protection to the birds you hope to attract. Chapter 5 lists many trees and bushes that are not only good cover but also provide food and winter shelter.

If you have room for it, a brush pile is a great attraction to many types of birds. Many birds like towhees and thrashers, who are at home scratching around in the brush in the forest, love to poke around in and under a brush pile. It also is excellent cover and, if made dense enough, can be winter shelter as well. A brush pile can be built in a corner of the yard from large strong branches on bottom for support covered with layers of smaller branches. Build it dense in the center with lots of leafy branches, but it should be open at bottom and top so the birds have lots of access to it. With the latest trend in landscaping being the natural look, brushpiles are not unsightly and will attract many birds especially woods-loving varieties.

Providing cover and considering its proximity when you locate feeders, birdbaths, and houses will make a difference, especially if you hope to attract some of the more shy, timid birds that are very wary about coming into a yard.


## DUST BATHS

You have probably seen sparrows bathing in the dust along the side of a road before. They shake about and flutter just as though they were in a birdbath. Many types of birds enjoy dust baths and providing for them can make for a lot of interesting viewing.

Experts differ in their explanations of why birds take dust baths. They say it discourages parasites; that is, it "drycleans" their feathers. Others say that they do it simply because they enjoy it. Because nearly all birds are infested to some degree with parasites, I will buy that explanation, but from just watching them at it, I think they enjoy it, too.

If you live in an area where sand is plentiful or in a dusty area, the birds around you probably have their own dust bathing areas all staked out. If you live in a built-up urban area with lots of grass and landscaping and few bare or dusty areas, however, a dust bath will be welcome. The simplest way to build one is to put together a shallow wooden tray about 3 feet by 4 feet, and 4 to 6 inches deep. Having the depth a bit on the deep side will save you having to fill the bath so often. Builder's sand, available at building supply stores, is very clean and inexpensive. It is packaged conveniently in 25-pound sacks and will last a long time. Any fine sand or dust will do the job nicely, however.

If you suspect that the birds that visit your dust bath are badly infested with parasites, there are a number of products available that can help. They come in powdered form at garden and farm supply shops, and they will kill nearly all common parasites. Most are inexpensive and packaged for easy application. They can simply be mixed with the regular dust in the dust bath using about 10 percent of the parasite killer. Because new products appear on the market all the time, the best source of advice on which to buy and how much to use is your vet, nurseryman, or farm supply dealer.

## NESTING MATERIALS

Nesting materials are needed every year by every nesting bird, whether in the construction of a whole new nest or in the renovation of an old one. Often, in our very clean yards and neighborhoods full of synthetic materials, it is hard for birds to find the kinds of materials they need. In the "old days" bits of straw and hay were used as well as horsehair, feathers, and snips of string and yarn. Today most of these things are not readily available and birds have to search over large areas to find suitable materials. Even rags and old bits of cloth have changed. Cotton was once the main fabric used. Now the old fabric scraps birds find are often synthetics that are hard to shape in the nest and impossible for them to ravel strings from.

Providing nesting materials is easy and gratifying. Nothing can be simpler than saving suitable scraps and making them available either on the ground, hung over branches or twigs, or on a feeder or nesting materials rack. Some things that make good nesting materials are: yarn, soft paint brush bristles (these take the place of the horsehair of old), scraps of thin paper, Spanish moss, thread, feathers, lint from the clothes dryer, small bits of cloth, straw, and unraveled string or soft rope. You will enjoy the busy work of the birds as they flit back and forth from their nesting sites to get more materials, and you can be sure that it helps them especially if there are many pairs of nesting birds competing for nesting materials in the same area.

I have examined some of the extras involved in attracting birds. Before going on to the actual feeder and birdhouse projects, let's look at some natural landscaping ideas that pay off, too.

# Chapter 5

# Plantings and
# Landscaping to Attract Birds

T HERE ARE MANY VARIETIES OF PLANTS THAT ARE NATU-
rally attractive to birds and are adaptable for use in your yard.
These plants provide food in the form of berries, fruits, or seeds
and also provide cover or shelter from bad weather. Many of them
are varieties of the same plants that serve birds well in nature. Using them as part of your landscaping scheme can provide you an
extra bonus in numbers of birds that visit.

Naturally attractive plants can lure birds to your yard who
might not otherwise come. For instance, a good stand of cedars
will certainly be spotted and visited by passing flocks of cedar waxwings. Berries will attract many types of birds to your yard during
the summer. Bright, funnel-shaped flowers are likely to attract hummingbirds. A knowledge of what birds are common in your area
and what plants make up their natural diets can help you decide
on plants to integrate into your landscaping.

## PLANNING AHEAD

It will take a little planning to get the maximum possible
benefits from this specialized landscaping. This will help you select
the kind of plants that attract birds successfully, grow well in your
area, and look pleasing in your yard.

The first thing I would advise is to do some plain old thinking
about which plants you might consider. Make a good list, not just
in your mind but actually on paper, of all the plants you can think

of that you might want to include. I would suggest including your favorite plants or those most familiar to you. Concentrate on what value they have, if any, in drawing birds to your yard. The following section will give you some ideas, too. Another source is your local nurseryman. I admit that most of the nurserymen I've have spoken with have been surprised that anyone would come to them for advice on how to attract birds; most folks come for advice on how to keep them away.

If you have any older people around experienced in attracting birds, gardening, or both, they are a wonderful source of information. This was brought home to me last year when I was trying to decide on a species of tree to fill a bare spot in the yard. The custodian where I teach knows how I enjoy the birds, and he suggested that I put in what is called locally a popcorn tree. I was not too much of a popcorn tree fan and told him so. He pointed to one across the campus. "Just watch the birds around that one all year," he said. I did just that, and what I saw convinced me that for my area, the popcorn tree is about the most valuable bird tree you could plant. In the spring, many species of birds came to feed on its tender buds. In summer, its open, airy structure made it a favorite perching place. In fall, as its berries swelled and ripened, it attracted more and more birds. By early January there were still seed pods left on the tree and sparrows, cardinals, warblers, towhees, finches, and even woodpeckers could be seen performing acrobatics as they clung to the tips of the branches trying to reach the seeds. I would never have guessed that this tree was so popular with birds, and this is just the type of information long-time residents can give you.

Even though you are trying to decide on plants that will attract birds, you don't want to overlook beauty. The next step, after getting together your list of possible bird-attracting additions to your yard, is to take a realistic look at what you need in the yard to make it attractive. Here all the standard landscaping rules apply. Try for good color balance, a variety of foliage textures and densities, and seasonal beauty. A walk around the yard helps because seeing the shape of any bare spots and the relationships between plants, buildings, sidewalks, etc., will help you plan better.

Be sure that you are planning for the future. Although we are usually impatient with the slow growth of the young plants we plant, wishing they were larger, showier, had bigger blooms, etc., it is important to keep in mind that if you are not careful in selecting and locating what you plant, you might have grief later on. The tiny maple that you plant on the side of the house might have to be cut down if you want to build the screen porch you talked about. The small bushes outside the door have an amazing way of quickly growing up and engulfing it. Try to think 5 to 10 years ahead and visualize what your yard will look like. Then pare down the plan again.

By this time, in addition to your list of possible plants, you also have an idea of where you will put them. If you haven't done it by now, make a sketch of your yard. Be sure to note fence lines, driveways, buildings, etc. Try for as close to a scale drawing as possible to be more able to see relative sizes of things. Include all existing bushes, trees, and flower beds that you intend to keep. I like to use a light colored pencil to shade in the shady or mostly shady areas, too, because that is a factor in deciding placement of new plants. I also include the location of all bird feeders, birdhouses, water sources, and ground feeding areas. In general, just include anything you might think pertinent in your landscape plan. Use the sketch to make final plans of which plants to include and where to locate them. Draw in plants and trees, look over the effect, and then erase it and try something new. For example, you will use it to decide on the proper color balance between flowering plants. You will want to try placing dense evergreen cover plants where they might serve as windbreaks for birds taking shelter there. More open cover plants can be planned to grow near where you locate your feeders as convenient resting places and lookouts. Plants attractive to hummingbirds can be sketched in near a window to allow for easy viewing. Spending a few hours mulling over your basic landscape plan will really help you make decisions you will be happy with.

There is another area of consideration for those of you who are really committed to developing the best possible environment for attracting birds—seasonal availability of foods and other benefits garden plants can give. If you are willing to take the time to research the plants available to you, you can ensure that at any season of the year your garden plants are providing the maximum number of benefits to your birds. You will be able to plan for early fruiting, midseason, and late fruiting food sources. You will learn which plants produce seeds or berries that remain on the plant far into the winter. You will arrange your yard so that at any season of the year there are plants that are providing cover and shelter.

This probably seems very complicated at first glance, but it is simpler than it looks. For example, in my yard I have some dewberry bushes. They fruit early in the summer. After they have fruited and are mostly eaten, the later blackberries begin to ripen. By choosing bushes, flowers, and trees that bear fruit, seeds, or berries at different times, I can provide at least some natural foods during most of the year. Even in January, there are usually a few cedarberries, haw apples, and popcorn tree pods left for the birds to pick over.

Make and use a landscape plan of some type. It will really help. When deciding which plants, bushes, and trees to include, don't forget that you really have many sources of advice. As I said, local gardeners and nurserymen can offer information. Other bird hobbyists often have valuable firsthand knowledge of which plants are favored by which species of birds just from their hours of observation. The following section will give you a bare bones outline of some good plants to consider. Finally, you also might want to think about which birds you want to attract, read about their diets and favorite foods (some are included at the end of Chapter 4) and try including plants that will provide for them. I do this every year when I plant a few sunflowers for the finches and cardinals that love them so much.

## FLOWERS THAT ATTRACT BIRDS

There are two main categories of flowers that are planted to attract birds; flowers that provide food and those used as cover plants. If you plan ahead for using them, they can be an integral part of your master landscaping plan. They also can be used to advantage in filling in empty areas in your yard. Naturally, you will have to analyze your own setup to decide which of these you might want to include. Some gardeners don't relish the thought of leaving seed-producing flowers in place long enough for the seeds to ripen. Others might not like the appearance of the garden after flocks of birds have pecked it over. These people can still allow for attracting birds naturally, however, by choosing as flower beds or decorative flowers those that will do double duty as cover plants, too.

Although this is only a partial list, some of the most popular flowers that produce seed that is eaten by wild birds are: petunia, phlox, 4 o'clock's, columbine, chrysanthemums, calendula, asters, cosmos, marigolds, zinnia, and verbena. You will notice that I have left sunflowers off the list, because as a bird food, they are in a class by themselves. Sunflowers are a favorite food of dozens of species of birds. If you have the room, a few of these giant plants can be dramatic in your garden. When the huge flower heads produce their masses of seeds, they can either be harvested or left right on the flower stalk for the birds to pick over naturally.

Nearly any densely packed flower plantings serve well as ground cover, but the taller they are, the more valuable they are. Shorter varieties of flowers don't allow the birds to hide as completely as taller ones do. Many birds have a tendency to feel very insecure on the ground. For them, taller flowers that they can perch among are better. Some of the best cover flowers are: princess feather, bellflower, chrysanthemums, columbine, pinks, cosmos, and portulaca. This is only a sampling. You will know which of your favorites can be used as cover. In addition, there are some flowers that give a natural, forest look, which is very popular in landscaping. Some of these are wildflowers, asters, black-eyed Susans, chicory, and the special, tall landscape grasses. All of these are especially good to use to fill in empty spaces in your landscaping plan and provide cover at the same time.

## SHRUBS AND VINES

Shrubs, bushes, and vines can serve as excellent cover, valuable food sources, and, in addition, they are very attractive to birds who prefer to nest at lower heights. Birds like cardinals are very happy nesting in a tall hedge or well established yard shrub. Conveniently placed shrubs are welcome cover in case birds are frightened from feeders or other areas.

There is such a variety in shrubs and vines that attract birds that you are certain to be able to include some in your landscape plan. Many of them produce lovely blossoms that will add to the beauty of your yard. Their seeds and berries are very good sources of natural foods. By learning a little about when they fruit and how long the fruit stays on the plant, you can arrange your shrub and vine plantings to provide food for many months of the year.

A sampling of the many valuable shrubs and vines must include elderberries, blueberries, buckthorn, blackberries, dewberries, serviceberries, bayberries, viburnum, wild raspberries, holly, hawthorne, honeysuckle, bittersweet, Virginia creeper, grapes, and greenbrier. This is the barest sampling because there are dozens of good candidates around. Depending on your part of the country, some or all of these might not be commonly cultivated plants. I have tried to pick a general list without regard for region. As suggested earlier in this chapter, there is no substitute for firsthand knowledge of local plants.

## TREES

Trees should be chosen for what they do for the beauty of your yard as well as for their attractiveness to birds. A nice combination of beauty and natural function can be realized if you take time to learn about bird diets and the food and shelter properties of various tree species.

Because most of wild birds' natural foods comes from trees, and many take shelter there in bad weather or to escape from enemies, and many types of birds nest and live in trees, the list of valuable landscaping additions is long. Once again, my list is very general, and many of the trees listed might not be common to your area. On the other hand, it is entirely likely that your local area supports a tree I have not even mentioned that is very beneficial to birds. Take this list as a stimulus to your own research.

Most of the following trees have been included in the list because of their superior shelter or food potential or both. At the top are beech and alder, which produce seeds relished by many birds. Ash is another good seed tree as is the birch. Wild cherry, crabapples, and cedar all produce welcome fruit of some form. Dogwoods are favorites wherever they grow as is the popcorn tree. Elms and maples are good nesting trees and sources of seeds. Firs, pines, and spruce are superior winter cover and provide food, too. Hackberry, hawthorn, and mulberry trees all produce fruit that ripens at different times of the year, making them easy to use to provide food sources throughout the year. Many birds enjoy acorns and rely on the oak trees that produce them. These are only a few of the trees you can consider for your landscaping.

## PLANTINGS TO ATTRACT HUMMINGBIRDS

For many people, hummingbirds are the most welcomed bird visitors they see. They are amazingly agile in flight as they hover and flit about. Hummers have a surprisingly large range throughout the country, and they are easily attracted to the proper environment.

Naturalists worked many years on field studies of hummingbirds to discover that what has been pretty obvious to any of us who live in a part of the country frequented by hummingbirds. Specifically, they found that although attracted to nearly any bright flowers, hummingbirds prefer brilliant red or orange tube or funnel-shaped blossoms. Naturalists also found that while many varieties are great travelers, often migrating thousands of miles, if the hummers find a ready source of acceptable flowers, they will spend a whole season nearby. They may, in fact, return year after year. Knowing these facts makes including some hummingbird-attracting plants in your landscaping scheme pretty inviting. After all, the hummers are beautiful and great to watch, and as luck would have it, the plants they are most attracted to are some of the loveliest.

There are many commercial hummingbird feeders on the market. Some are very good, while others are so ineffective and unattractive to hummingbirds as to be virtual ripoffs. Most come as plastic or glass tubes or cylinders that can be filled with a "nectar" either commercially available or easily made from a recipe. Many of them are fitted with red or orange blossoms that fit over the feeder and give it more of a natural flower look. Some are designed to hang freely suspended, but more commonly they are to be fixed to a tree or to a stick in the ground.

If you decide to use a commercial hummingbird feeder, you will want to place it so that it will not become totally infested with ants. This is pretty hard to do, ants being like they are, but give it a try. More serious problems are the squirrels who absolutely adore the sweet nectar in the feeders. One of my friends has an especially persistent squirrel who gets at the feeder just about anywhere she puts it. Often you can see him out there in the yard with his little paws on the feeder, tipping it up and drinking out of it as if he were a baby with his bottle.

Another problem for hummingbirds is cat predation. The sight of a hummingbird hovering nearly motionless in the air is like sending out a challenge to cats. This is a special problem if the food source that attracts the hummers is low to the ground. Plants like azaleas and gladiolas are low enough to force the little birds to fly down to where cats can reach them. The problem isn't usually as constant where the birds are attracted to the yard by taller plants and vines, but if you live with or near cats, you will have to expact cats to be a problem at times.

Some of the most common plants that attract hummingbirds are: columbines, azaleas, honeysuckle, tiger lilies, gladiolas, hollyhocks, coral vine, mimosa, trumpet vine bougainvillea, poinciana, fuchsias, shrimp plant, and jasmine. Look around and add to the list. The fun of watching hummingbirds is worth it.

Now that you have looked at natural landscaping for birds, let's go on with the building projects in Chapters 6, 7, and 8.

# Chapter 6

# Feeders

G ENERALLY, THE FIRST THING A PERSON DOES TO START attracting birds to his or her yard is to provide some sort of feeder. I have seen this pattern hold true for many different types of people under different circumstances. It just seems like the natural first step. After all, a food supply is guaranteed to bring the birds to the yard. Sometimes, too, the sight of birds out foraging in the cold and wet of winter sparks the idea.

Once a person decides that it is time to begin providing food, the next step is to choose a feeder design that will meet his needs. It is not really as simple as it sounds with the bewildering number of different types of feeders available. Should it be one of the cute little clear ones with the peaked roofs or the long, cylindrical, hopper-style seed feeder? Should there be provision for feeding foods other than seeds? Are homemade feeders more practical and versatile? All these questions deserve a good look. After all, the purchase or construction of a feeder that proves itself to be impractical or easily broken does not represent a budget breaking expense, but it is exasperating to go to the time and trouble to buy or build, install, and furnish a feeder that turns out to be a waste of your effort.

## WHAT TYPE OF FEEDER IS BEST FOR YOU?

Compared to what used to be available in the past, the variety of feeders I see on the market boggles the mind. There are commercial feeders in every department store catalog, in every discount store I walk into, and in every nursery or garden store in town. In addition, every veteran bird feeder has his or her own special homemade design. How is anyone without years of practical experience going to make a good choice?

## Commercial vs Homemade

The most basic decision to be made is simply, do you want to buy a prefabbed or fully constructed feeder, or will you be more comfortable building your own? There are advantages to both. Commercial feeders have the obvious advantage of needing very little in the way of assembly and installation. They are also available in a huge variety of designs, colors, and styles. There is sure to be one that suits your taste. They are available just about anywhere you shop as well as by mail order. There are even relatively expensive feeders, specially designed for certain types of food, available from conservation groups and specialty shops. Finally, most commercial feeders are made of materials that require very little maintenance.

The disadvantages of the commercial feeders often begin to show up when you start trying to establish a good, easily accessible food supply for a larger number of birds. Unfortunately, most of the feeders now on the market have been designed to appeal to people and not necessarily to birds. Most are cute and decorative enough to sell themselves right off the shelf and into your yard. Many times you will find commercial feeders with tiny little perching areas that many of the larger birds are not comfortable with or may not use. Often they are flimsy and bend or shake when birds land, scaring them until they get used to it. Most of the ones I have seen require unscrewing a top, sliding open a small filler hole, or even taking it completely down to fill. Because an established feeder will probably need to be filled daily, this is not very handy. Speaking of frequent filling, once you get a good population of birds at your feeder, you will see that most of the commercial feeders on the market only hold a quart or less of seed mix. That isn't very much considering that it is not uncommon for me to feed a 3-pound coffee can full of mix or more each day in the winter.

As you can surmise, I generally recommend homemade feeders. This is not to say that there are no good feeders on the market. In the past few years, and especially since the big, national plastic and rubber manufacturers have entered the market, there have been some really nice feeders produced. Even the less-than-perfect designs do very nicely for some people. One of the most active bird hobbyists I know uses two little round feeders that show just about all the features I noted above as disadvantages, and she would not change for the world. It is totally a matter of what fits you. If you are not especially handy in the shop or just don't have the time or desire to build your own feeders, then by all means shop carefully, compare features, and install your favorite commercial feeder. In fact, a very good combination is a commercial feeder to service the smaller birds with seed mix and a tray feeder for feeding other foods and serving larger birds or those who get crowded off the commercial one.

## Feeder Size

Feeder size is much more important than whether your feeder was homebuilt or came in kit or prebuilt form. In addition to the obvious problem of having to fill a small feeder much more often than a larger one, if your feeder is too small, larger birds will have great difficulty landing and perching on it. Small feeders can not serve as many birds at one time, either. This can lead to squabbles and birds flying off unfed. Many of the shier species will not approach a feeder crowded with others. Titmice and chickadees especially are so timid that they will wait on nearby branches for a time when the feeder is relatively clear of other birds. You will find that what often happens with small feeders is that a few boss birds will dominate the feeder as soon as they arrive and will trouble less aggressive birds to no end. All these reasons are cautions against having your feeder too small. Larger, easy-access feeders allow all the birds a better chance.

## Style of Feeder

The style of feeder you decide on has a lot to do with how usable it is to the birds around you. Remember that your main goal should not be how attractive the feeder looks in the yard but how practical it is. Look for a feeder with plenty of room for birds to perch. Beware of those that have perches molded in and placed about 3/4 to 1 inch from the food. Many of the medium or larger-sized birds simply can not use a perch so close. If you are considering a hopper type seed feeder, use caution. In most areas it gets wet enough, either from direct rain and snow or from humidity, to cause seed mix to swell and clog the hopper. This means frustration for you and for the birds. Be sure your hopper openings are large enough or sheltered enough to preclude that problem.

For most parts of the country the weather is severe enough at some times to make us consider using a covered feeder. Even for summer feeding a roof of some sort is handy. The problem is that a roof or cover is restrictive to you and to the birds. It restricts you because it makes it much harder for you to get a good look at whatever birds are visiting. Observing the birds and occasionally photographing them is one of the most enjoyable parts of the hobby to me. I don't personally prefer a covered feeder. In addition, covered feeders restrict the birds in approaching, landing, and perching on the feeder. Certain designs, those with one main opening, also make it possible for an aggressive boss bird to threaten away other approaching birds. If you live in snowy or extremely wet weather, my closest estimate to a happy medium concerning roofs on feeders is to build an open feeder with corner posts and a rather high roof. This should keep snow and most rain off the feed while allowing easy entrance and exit to birds and allowing you good visibility. Then I suggest a shelter box or three-sided, roofed shelter shelves placed around for birds to use to get in out of the weather.

With all the varied styles of feeders available, I can not analyze all of them. In general, after considering size and whether to choose a covered style, main pointers are: avoid anything that is difficult or awkward to fill. You won't want to grapple with a fancy screw-on cap or intricate slide-in tray early on a cold, wet morning. I have seen this sort of problem kill the desires of many a novice bird feeder. Remember that as the feeder ages, its material might shrink, flex, or become brittle or clogged with seeds making it much harder to operate. I like to avoid any feeder that requires me to carry along and fool with a funnel for filling. In my house, funnels have a way of disappearing at odd times. Look for openings that you can pour seed quickly and smoothly into. If there are children in your family, they are certain to want to help with the feeder. This is a great way to help a child learn the responsibility and the joy of doing a job all by himself. If a child is to have this opportunity, then consider your feeder style even more carefully to be sure a child can fill it.

## A Hanging Feeder or a Fixed One?

Here is another decision that can only be made by considering what the individual wants and is comfortable with. There are many feeder styles available for installation either of these ways. All I can do is offer a few comments.

You will find that hanging feeders are attractive to most species of birds, while the gentle swinging frightens others. In fact, I have encountered a few birds that simply would not use a swinging feeder. This has been rare, however, because most birds adapt nicely. You can lessen the swing of a hanging feeder by attaching a rather heavy weight to the bottom of it by a short length of chain. The weight will act as a counterbalance to stop the pendulum-like swing. Building your homebuilt feeder out of heavier than necessary materials so that it ends up weighing more will help lessen swing motion, too.

If squirrels and cats are a problem for you, a hanging feeder offers a good way to be able to avoid any chance of having one of these pests climb your feeder pole. Hanging it won't make your feeder cat or squirrel proof, but it may help. Just be sure to hang your feeder at least 8 to 10 feet from any roofs, fences, branches, or anything else a cat or squirrel can jump from. I have my feeders hung in trees in my yard about 8 feet off the ground. I have hung them from outer branches away from the trunk and main branches that are so easy to leap from. The tree branches are trimmed back to allow me to see the feeder and nearby resting branches. For filling and cleaning, the feeder is hung from a pulley with a rope running through it and down to a hook secured to the tree trunk. It is simple to unhook the rope, allowing the feeder to descend for filling. In order to keep it from falling all the way down, there is a knot positioned in the rope so that it hits the pulley to stop the feeder at about 4 feet from the ground. This arrangement, described in detail and with illustrations later in this chapter, keeps the feeders easily visible for me, easy to maintain, and as safe from cats and squirrels as I have been able to make them.

Feeders mounted on poles are attractive to many people. If they are mounted on metal poles so cats and squirrels cannot climb them, they are very practical, especially for locations without likely spots for hanging feeders. If you try to place the feeder high enough to prevent cats from jumping up onto it, however, it is probably going to be too high to fill quickly and easily. Keep in mind who will be filling it and how often it will have to be done. If your children are not going to be able to reach it to fill it or filling it will require a stepladder, you will want to consider that beforehand.

## Recommendations for Starting Out

My basic recommendation for a feeder to start out with has been made after lots of thought and trials. The choice I offer—a simple, open tray feeder—is not the most showy or intricate setup, but it is very easy to acquire, install, and maintain, and, best of all, it is virtually sure to be a successful bird attracter. In addition, it won't break, clog, or wear out easily over the long run.

The simple tray feeder has proved itself again and again. It is simple to build; just about anyone can make one. You can mount it on a pole or hang it. It is absolutely the fastest type to fill and clean. The open style makes it great for establishing your feeder initially, because the feed you offer will be spotted easily. Sometimes it takes weeks for birds to notice and begin to use other designs. A good-sized tray will accommodate large numbers of birds thereby lessening the competition squabbles common with feeders of more limited space. The larger size will also allow you to put out more food, so you don't have to fill it so often. Tray feeders make it possible to feed many different types of foods, too. You can offer different seed mixes, suet, and kitchen scraps. They are attractive to more species of birds than any feeders I have tried since their openness makes them seem secure to even the more timid birds. Being bigger makes it possible for large or small birds to use it. Some of the larger birds have a problem with smaller feeders and their tiny perches. I am so sold on tray feeders that it is the only style of seed feeder I use.

As for installing your feeder, I would have to recommend hanging it as I discussed earlier in this chapter. Hanging is simple, relatively safe from enemies, and less permanent. After all, as you gain experience, you might want to relocate the feeder. If it is installed on a securely-mounted pole, moving it will involve some digging and maybe some concrete work, too.

When all is said and done, a good-sized, simple, open tray should meet all the requirements you could set for a good first feeder. Even for those with lots of experience, a tray can offer a lot in terms of ease of maintenance and successful bird attraction. Take a look at the design later in this chapter and consider giving it a try.

## HOW MANY FEEDERS?

As soon as a small group of birds discovers your feeder and begins visiting it on a daily basis, your flock will begin to increase in number. Other birds flying by will see and hear feeding birds and drop in to check it out. It seems that the news of a secure, well-stocked feeder travels fast, and in a short time your feeding station will be crowded with hungry birds. When this happens, you will begin to see your first large-scale squabbles over a perching place on the feeder and over the feed itself. You will also begin to have disappointed birds from time to time who arrived too late and found all the feed gone.

The easiest way to cope with the competition problem is to provide more than one feeder. It isn't an expensive solution because an extra feeder isn't a big investment. An extra feeder allows you to accommodate the same number of birds or even more with fewer squabbles and fights. It also diminishes the problem of more aggressive birds taking over a feeder and keeping smaller, more timid species and individuals off. Sometimes whole species like titmice and chickadees disappear from your feeding flock after they are intimidated a few times by boss birds. Having an extra feeder may not solve the problem completely, but it helps if they have another food source to try. In my experience, it is a rare time that both feeders are occupied by aggressive birds. Most of the time, a bird can snatch a meal at one feeder or the other.

If you can manage it, try for two feeders in your yard. Using two different designs will provide for the varied feeding styles of several different species. For example, if your two designs are a hopper-type seed feeder and an open tray, the hopper will accommodate small seed eaters while discouraging larger birds due to its small perching area. The larger birds will be drawn to the easier perching on the open tray. The tray will be better for offering foods other than straight seed mixes, too. You can add suet, kitchen scraps, or fruit. In short, by doing a little planning about feeding styles and how to manage the bird population that you hope to attract, you can do a lot toward lessening the effects of crowding and competition.

While not exactly a "feeder," another way to manage your flock and alleviate crowding and competition is to use ground feeding. You can provide cheaper foods for ground feeding birds like doves and sparrows while keeping them from crowding the feeders at the same time. There is more on ground feeding in Chapter 2.

## FEEDER LOCATION

When you get ready to install your feeder or feeders, take a few minutes to survey your yard and think out all the angles of each prospective location. You might find that the spot you had all picked out for the feeder isn't the best location for it.

From the birds' point of view, they like a feeder that is located in a spot where there are nearby trees, powerlines, or tall bushes, so they can land there first and look the area over very carefully for enemies. The birds will be more secure if there is this kind of cover nearby. Once they are feeding, they can flit off to it if they are disturbed. The ideal site will be in full sun in the winter and partially shaded in the summer. It would be nice if your feeder could be sheltered from the cold north wind in winter by buildings, hedges, evergreens, etc.

Because cats and squirrels are bound to be a problem at some time or another, keep them in mind when you look for a location. The feeder should be far enough from fences and inviting branches so that these pests cannot use them to jump from. roofs are another staging area for leaping cats and squirrels. Squirrels think nothing of leaps of 8 to 10 feet, so it is tough to use location along as a preventative.

If you are looking for a place to hang your feeder, you will most likely decide on a tree branch. I will discuss my pulley method of hanging a feeder in the section on installation. Once you decide on a spot, you will probably want to do a little trimming on the tree. Cut back the branches that interfere with the smooth action of the rope and pulley, of course, but also cut back any large branches that grow out directly over the feeder. This will help discourage cats and squirrels. Choose a position along a branch that will allow your feeder to hang well out away from the trunk and main branches for the same reason. I hang my feeder by smooth nylon "ski" rope because it is slicker than natural rope and, therefore, harder for squirrels to climb. Using light chain is an invitation to squirrels to climb down it. Lastly, try for a spot where you can hang your feeder at least 6 feet high. I have seen my own tomcat jump up and catch a dove off a 5 foot high feeder, so I know this isn't too high.

Well, I have talked about where the birds would prefer the feeder to be and where cats and squirrels won't like it, but what about your own convenience? After all, the thing is going to be out there for you to enjoy, right? You will want to find a location in your yard where you can easily and comfortably spend time watching the antics of the birds. For many housewives, outside the kitchen window is a popular place so that they can watch the birds as they work. For others, having a feeder out in the open where they can view it from a patio door or breakfast nook window is ideal. I have one feeder in the front yard, because the living room window is a perfect viewing spot for me. Place the feeder so that you can see it. The other convenience factor is locating the feeder so that it is easy for you to fill the feeder. You may have a lovely site picked out off in a nice corner of your yard, but if you are going to have to shovel snow or dodge across 50 yards of raindrops to reach it and then stand there and fill it in the cold, you might want to reconsider. Choose a fairly close, fairly protected location, and here is a vote for having a feeder design that you can fill quickly and easily, without tools.

## INSTALLING YOUR FEEDER

Now that you have decided where you are going to locate your feeder, you will be eager to install it and let it start attracting birds for you. General guidelines for installation are pulled from plain old common sense. No matter how you decide to mount it, be sure it is mounted securely enough to allow for wind and weather as well as cat and squirrel assaults. Allow for easy maintenance and repairs. While it should be securely installed, be careful of making it so permanent that you cannot move it if you are unhappy with the location or want to relandscape.

Because the largest number of feeders are either hung or mounted on posts, I have devoted whole sections below to the ins and outs of installing them by those methods. If you have unusual circumstances and prefer to mount your feeder on the side of a fence or building, I urge you to investigate and take advantage of the vast number of clever specialty items now available in hardware stores. There are many different types of L-brackets that will serve well for mounting feeders against walls and fences, for example. Products like this, while not designed exactly for our hobby, really serve well in special cases. Most of the time there is a salesperson around who takes special interest in trying to solve interesting hardware needs. He will be able to show you products you didn't know existed.

### Installing Post and Pipe-Mounted Feeders

If your feeder is a commercial one designed to be post mounted, it will have a mounting method designed in. Your instruction booklet or box should explain how to attach it to a pipe or pole. If you build your own feeder or your commercial one does not allow for strong,

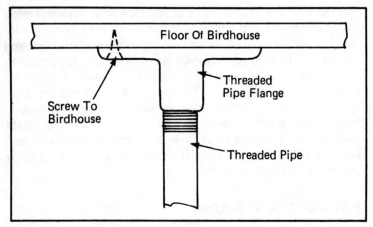

Fig. 6-1. Threaded pipe flange installation for pipe-mounted feeder.

convenient pole mounting, I suggest that you visit your hardware store and buy a pipe flange. A pipe flange screws onto the bottom of your feeder and is made so that a length of pipe can be mounted to it, either by threading it or securing it with set screws. See Figs. 6-1 and 6-2. Pipe flanges are commonly available and inexpensive. They come in a variety of pipe sizes.

Because I recommended pipe flanges, it is obvious that I also recommend installing your feeder on a metal pipe. Pipe has many advantages over wooden posts. It is more durable, of course, and not subject to rot or termites. It is slick so cats and squirrels cannot climb it. It is inexpensive, especially if you buy a length from

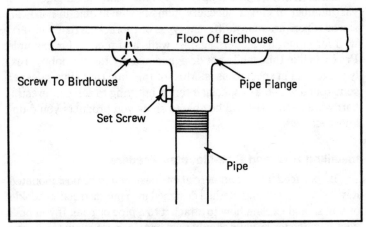

Fig. 6-2. Installation of pipe-mounted feeder using set screw type of pipe flange.

a discount store. It does not have to be the thickest, most expensive pipe, either, just so it is rigid enough not to bend and kink in a windstorm. I suggest unthreaded pipe and a flange designed for set screws because this makes it much easier to remove the feeder for repairs or replacement.

I tend to shy away from mounting feeders on wooden posts because they can be climbed so easily by cats and squirrels. If you prefer one or just have one lying around you would like to make use of, use a minimum of two angle brackets to extend up the side of the post and across the bottom of the feeder. See Fig. 6-3 for

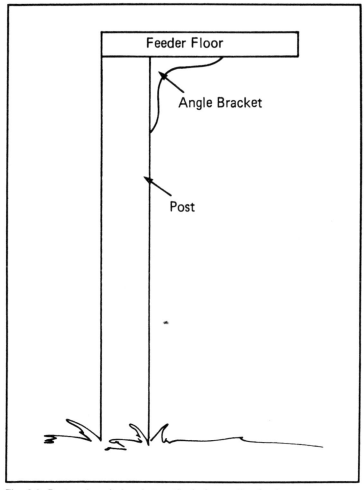

Fig. 6-3. Post-and-angle bracket method of mounting feeders.

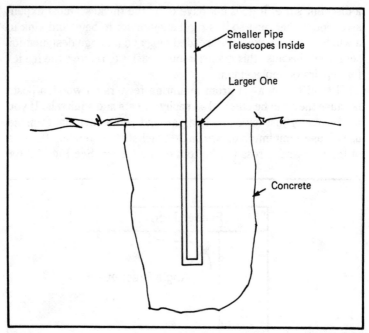

Fig. 6-4. Using telescoping pipe sizes allows for concreted-in security and easy removal of feeder and pipe.

an example. Using three brackets is even better. A wobbly, shaky feeder is not only less attractive to birds, but it is liable to work itself looser and looser as it gets blown around by the wind. As a finishing touch, you might want to take time to build a sheet metal cat and squirrel cone as shown in Fig. 6-20. One of these can really help keep pests from climbing up onto a feeder.

Whichever type of post you choose, I suggest you use concrete to install it securely unless you think there is a chance you will want to move it. If your feeder is going to be up for several years, it will be subjected to windstorms, bumps by lawnmowers and kids, and other stresses that can loosen a pipe or post that only has your natural yard soil around it. You might even want to consider concreting in a very short length of pipe, just to ground level, of a diameter that will allow your mounting pipe to slip snugly inside it. You will see what I mean in Fig. 6-4. This will give you the benefits of secure, concrete mounting and the ability to remove the pipe if you want to.

However you finally decide to install your post-mounted feeder, you will want to have it from 4 to 6 feet off the ground. I like about

5 feet because I am so aware of how high cats can jump. remember, the higher the feeders, the more difficult they are to reach for filling. You will have to think about a good height for your own feeder. If you have small children filling the feeder, it will have to be rather low. On the other hand, if you are taller than average, you can place it high enough to thwart cats.

## Installing Hanging Feeders

If your commercial feeder was designed for hanging, it will probably have an eyebolt or ring in the center of the top or roof. Check that it is strong enough to last through weather and other stresses and that it is made of a material that will not become brittle and crack with age. If you are unhappy with the hanger, take a look at the possibility of removing it and replacing it with a sturdy eyebolt, washer, and nut as shown in Fig. 6-5. Certain styles of feeders are hung from two eyebolts in the center of their roofs. For these, I suggest that you run a short length of light chain between the two. Then find a link from which the feeder will hang level, open the link by bending it with a pair of pliers, and attach a 1- or 2-inch ring. Your hanging rope can be attached to the ring. You can omit the ring, but it is really much easier to attach a rope to a ring than to a single link of chain. Without securing the rope to an individual link, you are bound to have it slip and tip the feeder. Figure 6-6 shows this arrangement.

Tray feeders take a little bit more work to hang. For square

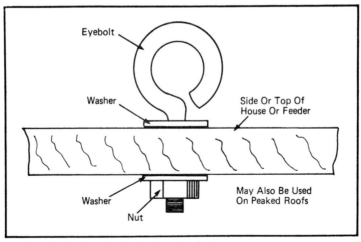

Fig. 6-5. Eyebolt installation for hanging feeders.

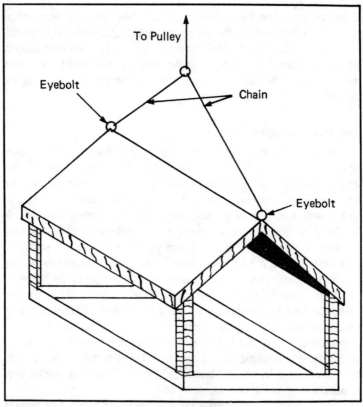

Fig. 6-6. Two-point method for hanging feeders.

or rectangular feeders, screw a screw eye into each corner. Be sure to choose one large enough to hold the weight of the feeder in all weather. If you prefer, eyebolts, washers, and nuts can be used. After you have installed the screw eyes, attach a short length of very light chain to each one. Usually 1 to 2 feet for each corner will do depending on the size of your feeder. Join all the lengths of chain in the center, about 12 to 18 inches above the feeder, by opening the links with pliers and ending them onto a 2- or 3-inch ring as shown in Fig. 6-7. Adjust the chain by trying different links until you have the feeder hanging level from the ring. The ring will be your point of attachment for the actual hanging rope or cord. Use the same general method for hanging round feeders. Three eyebolts around the edge will usually be enough to hang them securely.

I recommend that you use plastic or nylon "ski" rope to hang your feeders. It is inexpensive, available in many thicknesses, easy to work with, and lasts for years outdoors. It has the additional advantage of being slicker, which makes it harder for squirrels to climb. Natural rope will rot and wear outside season after season in the sun and wet. Chain will not run as well through a pulley and is easy for squirrels to climb. Attach the rope to the ring, and you are ready to hang the feeder.

The best way to hang your feeder is to use a pulley system. The pulley system allows for easy filling and maintenance. You can hang the feeder high enough to discourage cats from jumping up to it. This will allow you to keep the feeder at whatever height you choose while the birds feed. When you want to fill it, you are able to lower it down as low as you need it. A pulley system is not hard or expensive to make, and you will love the convenience.

Start by choosing the position on the tree where you want the

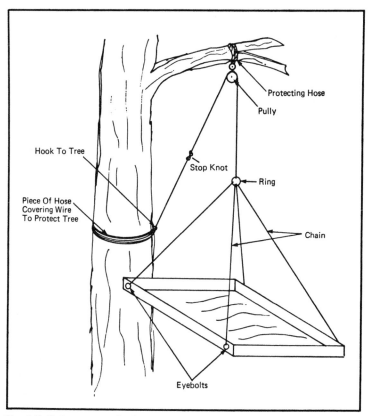

Fig. 6-7. Pulley system for hanging feeders.

feeder to hang. Protect the tree branch by cutting a short length from a piece of garden hose, slitting it lengthwise, opening it out flat, and placing it over the spot the feeder will be hung from. Run a strong wire, piece of rope, or a length of coat-hanger through the hanging ring of a one-loop pulley. Then tie or twist it in place securely over the garden hose around the tree branch as shown in Fig. 6-7. Now you have a pulley attached to an overhead branch with the branch protected against rubbing and chafing by the segment of garden hose. It is simply a matter of climbing up and running the free end of your hanging rope through the pulley and down.

You have to keep tension on the free end of the rope to keep the feeder from dropping to the ground. Work this to your advantage by attaching a hook to the trunk of the tree to which you can hook the free end. As you can see from Fig. 6-7, when I use the tree trunk, I wrap the trunk with old garden hose and run a length of coat-hanger wire through it and around the trunk. Where the two ends of the wire meet, I twist them into a downward-pointing hook. A ring or loop tied in the free end of the rope completes the setup. I can pull down on the free end to raise the feeder and hook it securely so that it stays up.

There is one last finishing touch to add. When you unhook the feeder and lower it, it will drop down just as far as you let it. In fact, it will go all the way to the ground. You have to hold tension on the rope while trying to fill the feeder, which can be inconvenient. To solve this problem, I decide during installation how low I want the feeder to drop and position a big knot in the rope so that it hits the pulley at the right spot to stop the feeder and keep it right where I want it. Now the system is complete.

Give this hanging system a try. I have had veteran bird feeders notice it and adapt it to their situations in many ways. It can be used for hanging feeders from porch eaves, too, or anywhere else you can think of.

## FEEDER MAINTENANCE AND CLEANING

Once your feeder is installed, there is very little maintenance to concern yourself with. Well-designed feeders seldom break, and if good materials were used in their construction, they seldom wear out. Your main concern will be with appearance and mounting. You might want to repaint the feeder as it weathers. I don't get too excited when my feeders develop a dull brownish-grey look, because I feel that birds will prefer the natural color. If you choose to repaint or revarnish your feeder, though, be sure to let it sit for a couple of weeks before you use it to allow the paint and varnish fumes to dissipate. More important are periodic checks to be sure your feeder is mounted securely. While sitting out there in the wind and storms, screws can work loose, wood can shrink and swell, and rope can rot and wear. Just make a quick visual check each time as you fill the feeder, and then every once in a while take a closer look for structural integrity.

As for cleaning, there isn't much to it, especially if your feeder is a well-designed one. For open tray feeders there is no waste to clean. The wind blows away all chaff and seed hulls, and, being exposed to rain, they stay surprisingly clean. The only time you really have to watch a tray is if you are feeding kitchen scraps. Any leftovers are liable to accumulate and possibly rot and draw insects. Other designs have their own special cleaning notes. Some hopper feeders are bad about clogging with swollen seeds in damp or wet weather. I have seen them absolutely full of wet, fermenting, and sprouting seed. It is a mess to clean. Keep an eye on your hopper, and if the seed level does not seem to be dropping as fast as usual, go out and look for a clog. Feeders with enclosed sides tend to have seed hulls and waste build up in the back corners. They occasionally need a scraping out and a good scrubbing with a brush. This is especially true if the feeder has been used for winter shelter as well as a feeding station. The ground under your feeders might need a raking occasionally, although I have not had a serious problem with accumulated seed hulls and bird droppings. What you will get is a lovely patch of sprouted bird seed foods. Sometimes the sunflowers, millet, and milo will sprout and grow much faster than your surrounding lawn. Then you get a dense green patch of rangy, grassy plants.

That is about the extent of normal maintenance and cleaning for feeders. Once again, the key to low maintenance is also the key to really successful bird attracting . . . that of choosing a design that is right for you, your local birds, and the type of involvement you want.

The feeders shown in this construction section were chosen to represent a wide choice of types, sizes, and degrees of difficulty. They are all proven, practical designs suitable for any part of the country and any local bird population. Hopefully there will be at least one feeder in the group that will appeal to you and be within your range of building skills, too.

## BASIC TRAY FEEDER

Tray feeders are just about the most versatile and successful types you could want, and they have the wonderful advantage of being the easiest to build, too. Consisting of only a bottom and four simple sides, they require minimal cutting, shaping, and fitting. Anyone who can nail the sides to the bottom and attach eyebolts

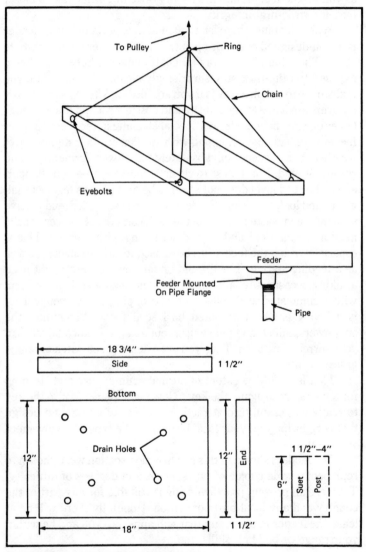

Fig. 6-8. Plan for the basic tray feeder.

- 3/8-inch plywood for end and side pieces.
- 1-inch stock (or other wood) for tray bottom.
- Scrap 1-inch stock for suet post (optional).
- Adhesive or glue (optional).
- 3/4-inch or 1-inch nails and /or screws (minimum of 18 to 20).
- 1/4-inch or 1/2-inch hardware cloth for suet cage (optional).
- Staples or small tacks for securing hardware cloth (opt.).
- 4 eyebolts and nuts (for hanging feeder).
- 8 to 10 feet of light chain (for hanging feeder).
- 1 1/2-inch or 2-inch ring (for hanging feeder).
- Pipe flange (for pipe-mounted feeder).
- Primer, paint, or stain, etc., as desired.

Fig. 6-9. Materials list for the basic tray feeder.

or a pipe flange for mounting can build one. They are an excellent first project for older children who are learning the basics of measuring and tool handling.

To start your tray feeder, the first step should be to assemble all the materials you will need. A look at the plan (Fig. 6-8) and the materials list for this project (Fig. 6-9) will help you be sure you have everything you will need. It is frustrating to get in the middle of a project and find you are short of screws or don't have enough wood. Remember that you will have to adjust some of these measurements if you are using wood of a different thickness than indicated.

Find the appropriate piece of wood and lay out the dimensions for the tray bottom. My favorite wood for this part of the feeder is 1-inch stock because it is easy to nail into, and it makes a heavier feeder—one that resists swinging too much in the wind. To get the 12-inch width, it is often necessary to join two 6-inch pieces with a flat screwplate or scrap wood, but it is worth the extra effort. Measure carefully and use a builder's square to get the corners as near 90 degrees as you can. Mark the wood and cut it out by using a hand saw, saber saw, or whatever you have. Give the edges a quick touch with rough sandpaper to smooth them, use about a 1/4-inch drill to bore several drain holes in it, and lay it aside. Measure the dimensions on your 3/8-inch plywood. Then cut out the two long sides and two shorter sides. Try for straight cuts that will let the corners butt flush against each other. You are ready to assemble the feeder now unless you are including a suet post. If so, go ahead and cut it out of scrap 1-inch stock. Note that the plans allow for either a small one for hanging a suet bag on or a wider one to which you can attach a bent-hardware cloth suet cage. Sand it as you did the bottom and sides, and lay it aside with the other pieces.

Spread adhesive on one of the shorter end pieces and butt it in place along one of the shorter sides of the tray bottom. Clamp or hold it in place and drill pilot holes for the screws, or, if you are nailing it, stand the tray bottom on edge so that you can nail through the side piece and into it. I recommend several nails or screws as the wood will shrink and swell with the weather. Repeat the process with the other end piece. Be sure you are placing the end pieces as nearly flush with the corner of the bottom piece as you can. If they overlap a bit, they must be sanded flush to allow the longer side pieces to fit properly.

Once your two end pieces are in place, you can use the same technique to attach the two side pieces. Fit them so they are as square as possible and be sure to apply plenty of glue to the ends of the end pieces, too, if you use it. Any minor gaps in your joints may have been filled with the glue already. If not, you can run a thick bead of it along the gap now to fill it completely. By the way, silicone sealant is a super gap filler because it is thick enough so that it does not run. Sand the whole feeder with rough and then finer sandpaper, and you are just about finished.

If you have included a suet post, let's work on installing it. If it is designed for a suet cage, take a piece of 1/4- or 1/2-inch hardware cloth a bit wider and shorter than the post and bend it out and around one side of it, squaring the corners. Bend the side edges of the hardware cloth so that it can be tacked onto either side of the post. Leave the top open for filling it with suet, but bend the bottom closed and tack it there, too. Stand the post where you want it on the tray bottom, and use a pencil to draw around it. Remove it and drill your pilot holes for two screws. Replace the post, stick the drill up through the pilot holes, and drill into the post bottom. Spread glue on the post bottom, line it up, and screw it in place securely. If you are using the smaller post designed for hanging a suet bag, all you need to do is lay it down and pound a nail into it that you can use to hang the bag on. Drill and attach it as for the larger one, but you will probably have to make do with only one screw since the post is smaller. With that done you are ready for the finishing touches.

The only finish I put on my feeders is a coat of clear, weather-proof varnish to seal the wood and preserve it. You might like to paint yours, however, as many people do. Sand the feeder until you are satisfied. Use a primer to seal the wood grain if you care to. Once this coat is dry and sanded, give it the final coat of paint. Whether you use paint or varnish, be sure to seal the insides of the drain holes, but don't allow them to become clogged. If they do, redrill them after the paint dries.

Final mounting comes now after the finish has dried. You have your choice of hanging this tray or mounting it on a post or wall. If you are going to hang it, drill holes in the side pieces near the corners for the four eyebolts and put them in using washers and nuts on the inside. Tighten them down snugly. Then attach 18 inches to 2 feet of light chain to each eyebolt by opening the end links of each one with pliers, running them through the eyes, and then rebending them. Bring all four chains together over the center of the feeder as high as you like, open the appropriate links, and attach them to a 1 1/2- or 2-inch ring. Play around with the lengths of the chains until you have the feeder hanging level at the right height. Close all the links tightly and attach your actual hanging rope to the ring.

If you are going to pipe-mount the feeder, center your pipe flange in the bottom of the feeder and screw it on securely. If you are worried about the strength of your tray bottom, you may choose to use bolts and nuts up through the bottom instead of wood screws. Then thread it onto your mounting pipe or use the set screws if you have that type of flange. Tray feeders can also be mounted using angle brackets if you are using a wooden post or mounting it to a wall or fence.


## PICTURE FRAME TRAY FEEDER

This particular design is the simplest tray feeder you can build with only one piece of wood to cut out and a minimum of hardware. It is a hanging feeder, perfect for any types of birds and any location.

The materials list is short for this project. The two big requirements are a picture frame of any size or type (although for trays in general the rule, is "the larger the better") and a piece of plywood or hardboard cut to fit the picture frame the way the glass ordinarily would. Most often an old frame can be found in the garage or attic, but if not, one can be bought in a discount store for very little. Try for a wooden frame because it is easier to screw the hanging hardware to. After the frame and wood, all you need is four small screw eyes, 4 or 5 feet of very light chain (or strong cord), a 2-inch metal ring, and some silicone sealant like bathtub caulk.

Once you have your frame, measure carefully and cut out the plywood or hardboard to fit inside the picture frame. If the original glass is intact, it is easiest to lay it on top of the wood and trace it. Trial fit the wood inside the tray after you sand its edges smooth. Once you are satisfied with the fit, run a bead of silicone sealant around the very edge of the wood, and lay it back in place. Top the edge with another bead to fill any crack between the frame and the wood. Allow the frame to dry several hours before you go on.

When the frame is dry enough to work with, lay it so that the flared lip of the frame faces up. This lip is what keeps the seed and other bird food from falling off the feeder or blowing away. It also forms a perching place for the birds as they flit to and from the feeder. Once you are sure you have it oriented right, screw in a screw eye at each corner. (If pilot holes are required, it is a job that an older person might do for a child who cannot handle power tools yet.) Divide the chain or cord into four fairly equal-sized lengths and attach one to each screw eye. The easiest way to do it is to use pliers to open the end link, slip it through the eye, and bend it closed again. Take hold of the four loose ends, hold them together over the feeder, and adjust their lengths until it is hanging straight and level. Thread the four ends onto the ring if the links will fit over it or open the links and rebend them over the ring as described above. Recheck to be sure the feeder hangs level.

Weatherproof your new feeder with a coat or two of varnish or paint. Be especially careful to thoroughly weatherproof it if you used hardboard or it will flake apart after a short time out in the weather. Once you have done that and given it time to air out, you are ready to attach a hanging rope to the central ring, hang it in a tree or from an eave, fill it, and enjoy it.

## COVERED TRAY FEEDER

If you want a feeder that offers more protection from the weather but still keeps the advantages of the basic tray, try this one. As you can see from the plan in Fig. 6-10, the roof keeps most of the snow and rain off the feed and the birds, while at the same time the feeder is still large enough to accommodate lots of birds, and it is open enough to allow you easy viewing and filling. It is versatile enough to be mounted on a pole or hung and is a sure bet for a successful feeder.

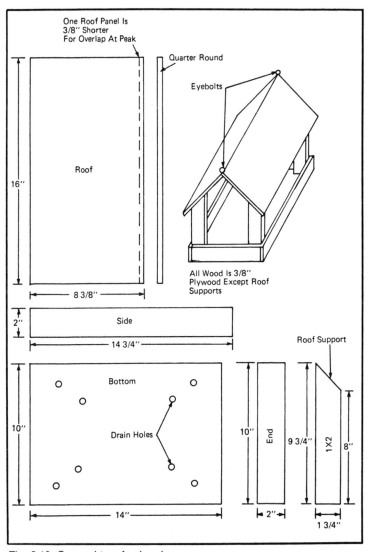

Fig. 6-10. Covered tray feeder plan.

The construction of this feeder has been kept as simple as possible. Start by laying out the dimensions for the bottom, four sides, and two roof pieces on your sheet of 3/8-inch plywood. (As indicated in the materials list (Fig. 6-11) for a heavier, sturdier feeder, use 1-inch stock for the bottom.) Mark the outlines of these pieces carefully, cut them out, give each a light sanding, and set them

- 3/8-inch plywood.
- 1-inch stock for bottom (optional).
- 1-by-2" stock for roof supports.
- 16 inches of quarter round stock.
- 1-inch screws (minimum of 16).
- 3/4-inch or 1-inch finishing nails (minimum of 30).
- Adhesive or glue (optional).
- 2 eyebolts and nuts (for hanging feeder).
- 2 feet of light chain (for hanging feeder).
- 1 1/2-inch or 2-inch ring (for hanging feeder).
- Pipe flange (for pipe-mounted feeder).
- Paint, stain, or other finish as desired.

Fig. 6-11. List of materials for the covered tray feeder.

aside. Cut your quarter round roof support out. Double check its
length against the length of the roof. It should be exactly the same
length. Be careful as you cut out the four corner posts. Notice that
the roof end of each one is cut at an angle. This is done by simply
marking the lengths on either side of each post and then drawing
a line between them for the cutting line. All the pieces can be given
a touch of sanding and laid aside.

The first step in the assembly of this feeder is to position the
posts. Trial fit them, being sure to have the roof bevels in the right
direction and each post squarely in the corner with no overlap.
When you are satisified, carefully drill pilot holes a size or two
smaller than the screws you are using. Apply adhesive to the bottom of each post and screw up through the bottom of the feeder
and into it. Try to use two screws in each post to prevent twisting,
but be careful; if your fasteners are too large, you will end up split-
ting the wood. At this stage, you have a bottom plank with four
corner posts firmly attached. Next come the sides.

Run a bead of adhesive (if you use it) along the two shorter
side pieces and butt them in place. Use very small finishing nails
to nail through the side pieces and into the bottom of the feeder.
Next, drill a pilot hole at each corner through the side piece and
into the corner post and screw in a wood screw. Use the same basic
technique to attach the two long sides to the feeder, although these
sides overlap the shorter ones on the ends. Take some time to go
ahead and drill several 1/4-inch drain holes in the bottom of the
feeder.

The roof is built with a straight 45-degree angle pitch. This is done very easily with your quarter round roof support. You will remember that one roof panel is 3/8 inch narrower than the other. Find that narrower panel and the roof support. Run a bead of adhesive along one side of the roof support. Use very small nails to attach the panel to the roof support with the edges even. Next, apply adhesive to the other side of the roof support and nail the wider roof panel to it so that the edge of the second roof panel overlaps and butts against the first one as shown on the plan drawing. You should have the roof unit ready to install now. Simply line it up on the posts, drill pilot holes down through it, and screw it in place.

Because part of this feeder is plywood, it will have to be weatherproofed with paint or varnish. Be sure to choose a product that will not be toxic if birds peck some of it off while feeding. All that remains is to mount or hang it. You can use a standard pipe flange on the bottom if you plan to pipe-mount it or angle brackets for a post or against-a-fence-or-building installation. If you choose to hang it, fasten two eyebolts through the roof as shown on the plan drawing, and hang it as described earlier in this chapter in the section on installing feeders.

## HOPPER FEEDER

This hopper, shown in Fig. 6-12, is designed to be post or wall mounted, but it may be hung as well. Its large capacity should keep your neighborhood birds well fed without constant refilling, and the roomy "porch" allows several birds to feed at once.

Look over the materials list (Fig. 6-13) for this feeder and then begin by measuring and cutting out all the parts you will need. Measure especially carefully on the two side pieces because of their unusual shapes. Once the parts are cut out, sand them lightly and gather together everything you will need for the actual assembly.

Notice that the glass and the back piece both fit inside the side pieces. Your first step will be to stand the back piece on its side edge and glue and nail or screw a side piece to it. Turn the piece over and do the same for the other side. Now you have a basic shell in which to install the glass. You will need two 3/4-inch scrap spacers to help you establish the gap needed at the bottom of the feeder. Without this gap, the food won't be able to flow out. Trial fit the glass by positioning the top of the glass even with the top of the side pieces and using your scrap spacers to keep it 3/4 inch above the bottom. The edges of the glass should be flush with the

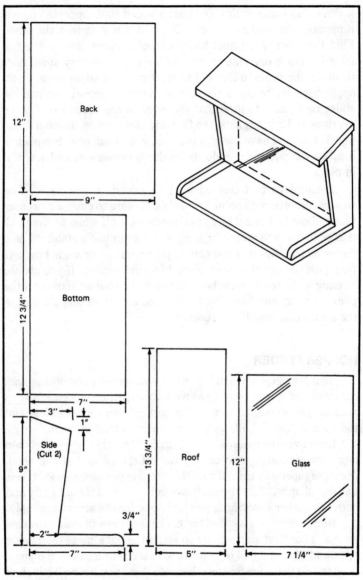

Fig. 6-12. Plan for the hopper feeder.

front edges of the side pieces. When you are satisfied that everything fits well, remove the glass and run a generous bead of silicone sealant along the inside front edge of the two side pieces where the glass will seat. Gently spread the two side pieces apart and nestle the glass in place, bedding it well into the silicone. Be sure you are using the spacers to hold the gap at the bottom. Clean up the silicone if necessary to make a neat joint, and then use several large rubber bands or tape to hold the glass firmly in place while the silicone sealant cures. Once it is firm, examine the joint carefully, and, if you think it needs it, run another bead of silicone along the inside of the feeder. Silicone adhesives are strong as proven by their use in holding together aquariums, but it is better to be safe than sorry.

All you have left to attach are the bottom and the roof. For the bottom, simply turn the feeder over, apply a bead of adhesive to the bottom edges of the back piece and both side pieces, and then screw or nail it in place. Be careful about putting too much pressure on the unsupported parts of the side pieces while nailing or screwing the bottom on. The roof is easy, too. Trial fit it. Make sure you are allowing for the large overhang in front and the 1/2-inch overhang on each side. Then hinge it to the back of the feeder so that it opens wide for easy filling.

Time for the final touches and then mounting. Because this feeder will have to withstand seasons outdoors, it will have to be weatherproofed. Use whatever finishing method you like—plain varnish, primer and paint, etc. Add hooks and eyes or other fasteners to each side to hold the roof down snugly, especially if you plan to hang the feeder. I often omit them on pole or pipe mounted versions since the weight of the roof itself usually keeps it closed. Allow the feeder to air out for a couple of weeks, and then it is ready to mount and fill. If you are mounting it to a metal pipe, the standard pipe flange method is simple and secure. Angle brackets work nice-

---

- 3/8-inch plywood.
- Glass or plexiglass, 1/4-inch thick, 12- by 7 1/4-inches.
- Silicone bathtub caulk-type adhesive.
- 1-inch stock scraps for use as spacers (minimum of 2).
- 3/4-inch or 1-inch finishing nails or small screws (minimum of 20).
- 2 small hinges.
- 2 small fasteners (hooks and eyes, etc.)
- 1 eyebolt and nut set (for hanging feeder).
- Angle bracket or pipe flange (for post or pipe-mounted feeder).
- Paint, varnish, or other finish as desired.

Fig. 6-13. Materials list for the hopper feeder.

ly for mounting it to a wooden post or against a wall, tree, or fence. For hanging it, make sure your roof hold-down fasteners are strong, and then install an eyebolt through the roof, centered lengthwise and toward the back. Attach the hanging rope to the eyebolt with a swivel-snap fastener like those you find on dog leashes. When it comes time for filling, you can either just raise the feeder to give the rope some slack, and then open the roof, or you can unhook the swivel-snap fastener and remove the feeder altogether.

## EASY-TO-MAKE HOPPER FEEDER

This free-flowing hopper-style feeder, shown in Fig. 6-14, is not only easy to make but also one of the least expensive projects. The only materials necessary are a 12-inch square piece of scrap wood, 4 feet of quarter-round molding, a tiny piece of scrap wood stock, a long nut and bolt, an eyebolt and nut, some glue and/or small nails or tacks, and an empty plastic shampoo bottle. In a pinch, you can modify the platform size to fit any piece of scrap wood you have or even use an inexpensive metal pie pan instead.

Begin by finding a 16-ounce (or larger) plastic shampoo bottle and its cap. Try to choose one of the semitransparent ones that you will be able to see the level of the seeds inside from a distance. Although any type of cap will do, it is more difficult to use one of the flip-top types. The plain screw-on caps are much better. Wash the bottle and cap out thoroughly as any trace of shampoo scent or taste will discourage birds in a hurry. Sit the bottle upright and use a felt tip pen or crayon to sketch three evenly-spaced openings around the base. The openings should be about 3/4 inch square to allow for good seed flow. Cut them out using a sharp knife like an X-Acto knife. Drill a hole through the center of the top of the bottle cap the correct size for the eyebolt. Bolt it in place with the nut on the inside. Trial fit the cap back in place. Caps vary with regard to how much clearance they allow on the inside. The eyebolt might extend down into the neck of the bottle, not reach it at all, or, especially if the eyebolt was not centered well, it might interfere with screwing on the cap. The first two cases, of course, are to be desired. If the eyebolt interferes, you might find that you can still screw the cap on far enough to hold. Be careful here, though, because you don't want it to work its way loose during windy weather and spill all your seed. If you cannot cap the bottle tightly, you will have to try a smaller eyebolt, one that will fit down into the bottle neck, or you can try to recenter and redrill it. At

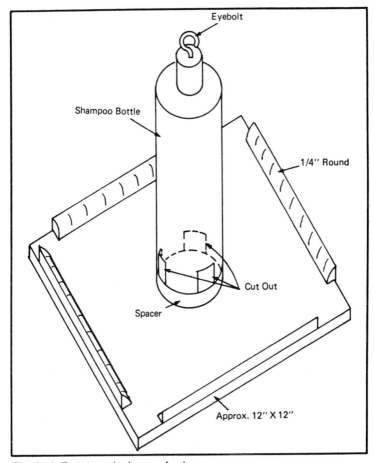

Fig. 6-14. Easy-to-make hopper feeder.

any rate, once you are satisfied with the hopper holes in the bottle and the eyebolt in the cap, you are ready to work on the seed tray.

Although I specify a 12-inch square seed platform, any size scrap stock will do. Try not to get the platform smaller than about 8 inches square, however, or you will not have enough room to accommodate more than a few small birds at one time. The shape does not have to be square, either. Rectangles are fine as are any shapes with edges straight enough to fix the quarter-round molding to. Because this is a light-weight structure, supported only by the eyebolt in a plastic cap, try to opt for lighter stock for the seed platform. Thinner plywood is a better choice than heavy 1-inch stock.

Once you have settled on a seed platform, sand the roughness off the edges and measure your quarter-round molding to fit. Note here that although I indicated 4 feet of molding, if you modify the size of the seed platform, you may need more or less than that amount. The purpose of the molding is to provide a perching place for small birds and to keep the accumulated seeds from falling off the feeder and being lost in the grass below. You don't want to run the molding completely around the platform, however, or you will end up with a shallow lake of rainwater during storms. To provide for good, no-clog drainage, cut your edge molding so that it only comes to within 1 inch of each corner. Sand the molding as necessary and use glue, silicone sealant, and/or small nails or tacks to hold it in place along the edges. Lining up the molding neatly and flush will make a prettier finished product.

If you decided on a metal pie pan for the seed platform, you won't have to worry about molding edges, of course, but you will have to drill several drainage holes in the bottom. I prefer wood because it is not so cold or slippery for the birds, but a pie pan is a quick and easy platform. Please don't try to make do with a thin, disposable pie pan, though. These pans don't last long enough to be worth your time.

Now you are ready for final assembly. Center the bottle on the platform, and when you are satisfied with the position, draw around its base. Try to center it as best you can, or it will be unbalanced and tend to hand crooked. Find a small piece of scrap 1-inch stock (1-inch stock actually measure 3/4 inch thick) and cut it so that it fits under the base of the bottle as shown on the plan. This spacer raises the hopper above the level of the platform to allow for better seed flow and to keep it above any accumulated water. It should not stick out beyond the base of the bottle much if any, or it may hamper the flow. Center the spacer over the drawing of the base that you made on the platform and drill down through both spacer and platform to allow for the nut and bolt. Next find the center of the bottle base and drill it, too. Place the screw on the tip of a screwdriver, and, holding the bottle upside down, work the screw and screwdriver into the bottle and into the hole from the inside. It is tricky, and it may require a very long screwdriver. Once you have the screw in place, sticking out of the base of the bottle, simply run it through the spacer, through the plattorm, and screw the nut tightly in place on the bottom. For added security, I recommend a good dab of silicone sealant (bathtub caulk is perfect) between the base and the spacer and between the spacer and the platform. Then go ahead and seal the nut in place. If you don't have a screwdriver long enough to tackle screwing the bottle in place, a generous application of silicone sealant acts as a perfect adhesive and withstands years of weather. Simply glue the parts together instead.

The final touches to this project are simple. You will have to weatherproof all wooden parts, especially if you used plywood. This can be done with a coat or two of varnish or paint. I don't recommend painting the hopper itself since you want to be able to see through the semitransparent plastic bottle to judge how much seed is left inside. Let the paint or varnish fumes dissipate for a couple of weeks and then go over the feeder checking to be sure that all the parts are well attached and strong. Remove the cap, use a funnel to fill it with seed mix, and then hang it from an eave or tree branch. Make sure it is low enough so that you can reach it easily for refilling. If you want it higher than you can reach, and that is an excellent idea if there are cats or other natural enemies around, refer back to the pulley system for hanging a feeder. A pulley system allows you to keep the feeder high but still easy to service when you need it.

By its very nature, a hopper feeder requires a little more attention than an open tray or some other styles. Because the seed is channeled through three small openings, clogs are more common than with other styles. Chunky seeds or foreign matter in the seed mix are often the culprits here. For my hoppers, I use only mixes containing small seeds like millet and milo. I don't include sunflower seeds, corn, or other bulkier foods. If you use a commercial mix, it will probably have sunflower seeds in it. Go ahead and use it in the hopper, but keep a watch on it. The other thing that leads to hopper clogs is damp, wet weather. It is surprising how much seeds can swell once they get wet. The spacer in this design keeps the hopper raised to avoid this somewhat. Generally, the birds eat the seed fast enough to keep it free running, but keep an extra watch on it during wet weather. One year I got busy and didn't pay attention to my hopper for several days. It was summer, and there weren't many birds using it, so I wasn't surprised that the level was barely dropping at all. When I finally took a close look at it, I found that the seed had gotten wet, swelled, clogged the feeder, and it began to sprout, rot, and ferment inside. It was mess! So take my advice and check your hopper feeders frequently.

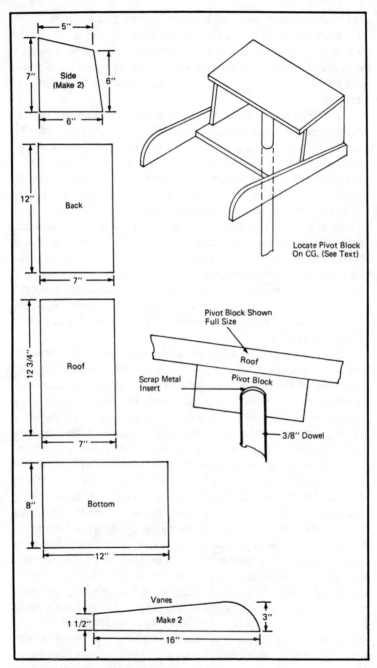

5″

7″  Side
(Make 2)  6″

6″

12″  Back

7″

12 3/4″  Roof

7″

8″  Bottom

12″

Locate Pivot Block
On CG. (See Text)

Pivot Block Shown
Full Size

Roof

Scrap Metal
Insert  Pivot Block

3/8″ Dowel

Vanes
Make 2

1 1/2″  3″

16″

Fig. 6-15. Weathervane feeder plan.

## WEATHERVANE FEEDER

The weathervane feeder, in one variation or another, has been around for many years and is a favorite of many bird hobbyists. Because it swings around to keep its back to the wind, it offers lots of protection from cold winds, snow, and rain. In the cold of winter, birds often crowd onto them for shelter even when there is no food available. They are versatile, too, because you can feed seed mix, kitchen scraps, suet, or any combination of these foods from them.

Before you begin, look over the weathervane feeder plan (Fig. 6-15) and the materials list for it (Fig. 6-16). Then measure and cut out the seven pieces that make up the feeder, sand them lightly, and lay them aside. You will begin assembling the feeder by standing the bottom piece on one of its long edges and positioning the back over it. Be sure the two pieces are flush. Apply glue, if you use it, and nail or screw the back piece to the bottom. Stand this unit on end and line up one of the side pieces. Glue and nail or screw it in place, too, and then attach the other side piece in the same way. All that remains of the basic shelter is the roof. Line it up, allowing for the overhang in front and on each side, and glue and nail or screw it in place.

Attach one of the vanes by overlapping it over the side piece until it is flush with the bottom and back edges. Line it up carefully and drill through both the vane and the side piece in two places. Use bolts, washers, and nuts to hold it securely in place. Attach the other vane in the same way. The basic shell of the feeder is finished now.

---

- 3/8-inch plywood.
- 1-inch stock scrap (for pivot block).
- 3/4-inch or 1-inch finishing nails or small screws (minimum of 30).
- 2 feet of 3/8-inch dowel.
- Small scrap of metal (as from can lid).
- 1-inch long bolts with nuts and washers (4 sets).
- Two 1-inch wood screws (for attaching pivot block).
- Glue or other adhesive (optional).
- Paint or other finish as desired.

---

Fig. 6-16. List of materials for the weathervane feeder.

In order for the feeder to pivot and face away from the wind, you have to place the pivot block, shown on the plan, as near the exact center of gravity as you can. Otherwise, your feeder may not behave as you would like it to. To find the center of gravity (CG), take a short pencil or section of dowel and place it inside the feeder against the roof and toward the front center. Balance the feeder on the pencil in several spots until you find the one where it balances best. Mark that spot because for our purposes that is the CG. Next, we have to mark the location for the hole through the bottom of the house. To get it directly under the CG spot, make a tiny plumb bob by tying a small weight to a string and tack it to the CG spot so that the weight hangs down to very near the bottom of the feeder. (Be sure the feeder is level.) Mark the spot under the weight, and you have the position for the bottom dowel hole. Go ahead and drill it, but it is important that you do not make the hole too tight a fit or the dowel will bind and not pivot freely, especially as the wood swells in damp weather.

It is time to drill the pivot block, but you will notice that it will be fastened to the inside of the roof. That means that it will not be parallel to the floor of the feeder but on an angle to it instead. If you lay the block on your workbench and drill it for the dowel you are likely to end up with the hole at the wrong angle. (See what I mean about the angled hole by looking again at the plan.) To mark the proper drill path, take the pivot block and position it on the *outside* of the side up under the roof overhang. Place it as close to the proper distance in from the front as you can, and then hold the dowel against it as though it was in its proper place. Allow the dowel to overlap the pivot block about 1/2 inch because that will be the approximate depth of the hole. When you have everything lined up as much like the actual positioning as possible, draw around the dowel, and you should have an accurate drill path.

Drill the pivot hole carefully, and then find a small piece of metal that will fit into the bottom of the hole. A piece snipped from a can works well. The purpose for the metal hole liner is to give the dowel a smooth, hard surface to turn on. A small amount of weatherproof glue like epoxy or silicone adhesive will keep it in the hole. Position the pivot block inside the feeder again so that the hole is as close to being over the CG spot as you can get it and draw around it. Drill pilot holes through the roof and into the pivot block, apply glue to the block, and screw it in place. Now it is time to take a knife and slightly round the tip of the 3/8-inch dowel and then coat it with bar soap. The soap will act as a lubricant. Now when you insert the dowel you should find that the feeder turns very freely and with little force needed.

Finish the feeder as you like using primer and paint, stain and varnish, or any favorite method. Allow it to air for a couple of weeks, and then install it. If you are going to mount it on a wooden post, all you ave to do is drill a 3/8-inch hole several inches deep and seat the dowel in it. If you prefer a pipe mount to discourage cats and squirrels from climbing it, you can take a length of 2 × 4 or 4 × 4 and bore a hole in one end of it large enough to allow it to slip over the end of the pipe, and a 3/8-inch hole in the other end for the dowel.

## LOG FEEDER

Log feeders like the one in Fig. 6-17 are rustic-looking ways

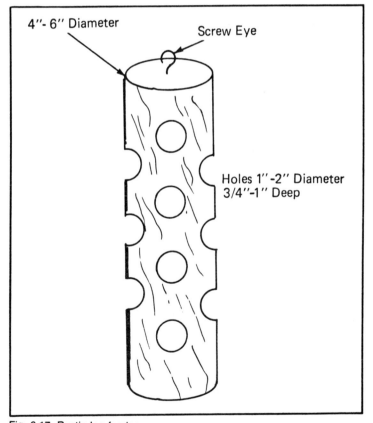

Fig. 6-17. Rustic log feeder.

to supply peanut butter or suet to your birds. They are easy and quick to build, and they are old favorites for many people.

A suitable log for this project is straight, about 4 to 6 inches in diameter. Downed trees in the woods or cut firewood are good. Trim off any small branches or other large irregularities as well as loose bark. Take a look at the two ends of the log and if they are jagged or crooked, saw them off straight. Use a wood bit to bore the holes on the sides. Wood bits come in various sizes with adjustable ones in sizes up to and over 2 inches. If you don't have a bit like this, you can use a sharp chisel and a hammer to cut out square holes instead. About 3/4 to 1 inch is the proper depth depending on the thickness of the log. Be careful not to end up with your holes directly opposite each other because this weakens the log. stagger them up and around the sides instead.

Once you have the holes bored or cut, drill a pilot hole about two sizes smaller than your screw eye as nearly centered in the top of the log as possible. Centering the screw eye will help insure that the log hangs straight. Now you are ready to fill the log with semisolid melted suet, peanut butter, or treefood (there are recipes for treefood in Chapter 8). Once that is done, you are ready to hang it. Of course, because you will have to remove the log frequently to refill it, be sure that you hang it from a rope that has a hook on the end. I have had good luck attaching a swivel snap clip, like the ones you find on dog leashes, to the hanging rope. It hooks and unhooks quickly and won't come open during a windstorm.

### SUET FEEDER

This suet feeder, shown in Fig. 6-18, is quick to build and great for holding larger amounts of suet. As you can see from the materials list (Fig. 6-19), it is built of sturdy materials and designed to offer more durability than a suet bag. You will find that a separate feeding place for suet eaters not only keeps your seed feeders less congested, but it also allows shyer birds who might not visit a busy, all-purpose feeder a chance. This type of feeder is especially attractive to tree-loving birds like woodpeckers and chickadees, because you can mount it right against a tree.

There are only eight simple pieces to cut out for this project. Measure for each one, cut them out, and sand them lightly. Snip out the hardware cloth, measure and mark 1/2 inch in from either side, and bend straight creases to form right angles. You should end up with a 5- × -5-inch square of hardware cloth with little 1/2-inch sides sticking up.

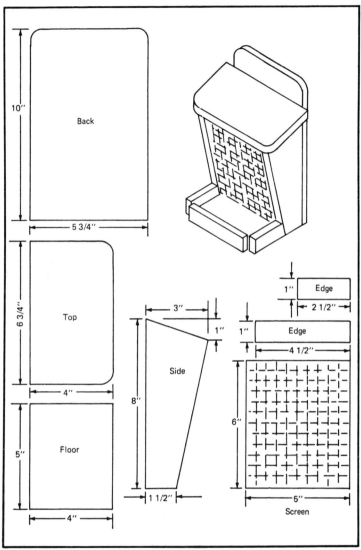

Fig. 6-18. Plan for the suet feeder.

Lay one of the two side pieces on its side and fit one of the 1/2-inch sides of the hardware cloth against its inside. The wire should be flush with the front edge of the side piece and positioned to leave a 3/4-inch space at what will be the bottom. Use several tacks or staples to attach it. Turn the whole thing over and attach the cloth to the other side piece in the same way. When this

- 3/8-inch cedar, cypress, or redwood fencing board (or 3/8-inch plywood).
- 5-by 6 inch piece of 1/2-inch hardware cloth.
- Glue or other adhesive (optional).
- 3/4-inch or 1-inch finishing nails or small screws (minimum of 30).
- Staples or small tacks (minimum of 15).
- 2 small hinges.
- Stain, paint, or other finish (optional, or if plywood is used).

Fig. 6-19. Materials list for the suet feeder.

step is finished, you will have the two side pieces joined by the hardware cloth across the front. Place the floor between the two sides and glue and nail it in place flush with the back edges of the side pieces. Next, fit the back piece on and glue and nail or screw through it and into the sides and floor. Be sure to allow the back piece to stick up above the top of the side pieces. Trial fit the three floor rails, noting that they do not meet at the corners. This is to allow for good drainage. Glue and nail them on. All that remains is the roof, which can be trial fitted and then attached by using small hinges at either side. The hinged roof will enable you to resupply the feeder quickly and easily no matter how large your suet chunks may be.

If you have used redwood, cedar, or cypress fence stock, you have no finishing to worry about. If you have built this feeder of plywood, give it a coat or two of paint or varnish to protect it. When it is time to mount it, you can nail or screw through the extended part of the back. You can also drill two holes and lace rope or wire through them to it and around a tree or post. For flush mounting you can use angle brackets. However you decide to mount it, if you keep this suet feeder well filled, it will be winner for you.

## CAT AND SQUIRREL DETERRENT CONE

If you are troubled by cats and squirrels climbing bird feeder or house posts, you may want to try a cone like the one shown in Fig. 6-20. Simple to build, they are very effective against cats and most squirrels.

All you need for this project is some thin sheet metal and pop rivets or small nuts and bolts to join the edges. You may even want to solder it instead. Begin by drawing out a half circle with a 25-inch radius on your piece of sheet metal. Use tin snips to cut it out and lay it flat on your work table. Next, measure the diameter of the post you are trying to protect. That number will be the size of the bend radius of the cone. Find the center of the side of the half circle and draw out your bend radius with a felt tip pen or crayon. Then subtract 1 1/2 inches and mark the cut radius. Go ahead and cut along the cut radius. Then take your tin snips and make several snips in from the cutout to your bend radius line. Try for about 10 to 12 evenly spaced cuts to be sure the cone ends around the post smoothly. Bend these "tabs" upward. You will nail or screw through them later to keep the cone in place. Trial fit the cone around the post now, bending it as needed to overlap neatly. You may need to trim and bend the tabs to be sure the cone is going to fit. If it is too snug, simply remove it and deepen and rebend each of the tab cuts a bit until it is the proper size. You should be able to slide the cone up and down the post. Once you are satisfied, even up the overlap on the cone edges, and, with the cone in place around the post, drill and pop rivet or bolt it together, or you can solder it. The advantage to solder is that if you file down the edges afterward, there are no bolts or other rough edges for squirrels to use for climbing.

Now you are ready to decide on the cone's final position on the post. Slide it up the post until you have it at a height where a cat or squirrel won't be able to leap from the ground and clear it. If

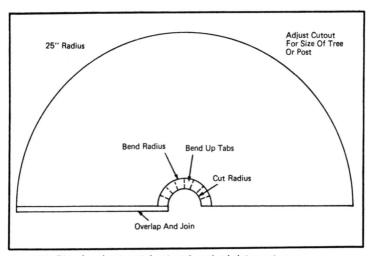

Fig. 6-20. Plan for sheet metal cat and squirrel deterrent cone.

it is too low, the animal will simply jump over it. A better position is high enough so that the cat or squirrel has to climb the post and then try to climb over the slick cone, too. When you are happy with the height, nail or screw through the tabs and into the post, and you are all set.

# Chapter 7

# Birdhouses

THE UNITED STATES FISH AND WILDLIFE SERVICE ESTIMATES that there are more than 50 species of common birds in the United States that will occupy birdhouses. These are birds in all areas of the country and all habitats from urban to rural. Just about anywhere you care to put up a birdhouse, there will be a type of bird to occupy it. Maybe that is one of the reasons birdhouses have been so popular for so many years.

Like bird feeding, the pastime of providing birdhouses is currently enjoying a huge jump in popularity. More people are involved than ever before in activities that range from putting up a martin house in the yard to establishing a bluebird trail in the woods. Merchants all over the country are rushing to stock the latest houses and kits, especially since the larger plastics products companies are re-entering the market with high quality and a variety of designs. Of course, I am glad to see more people and businesses in the hobby, but it can tend to make things a little confusing when you try to decide what type, number, and design of birdhouse to choose.

## WHAT TYPE OF HOUSE?

There is one absolutely cardinal rule to follow when deciding what type of birdhouse is best for you; that is, be sure to plan ahead and choose a house that is designed for the type of bird you are trying to attract. No matter what the advertising says about a house being "universal" or attracting "any" type of bird, don't believe it. Experts have devoted years of research to finding out exactly which species of bird prefers which type and size of house, how large the opening should be, how far the opening should be above the floor, and other very specific facts. You simply won't be as successful if you don't plan ahead and follow the specifications.

In order to take advantage of all this information, it makes sense that you have to get some idea of which birds you can reasonably hope to attract to your yard. If you already have established bird feeders, you probably have one or more species visiting them that will use birdhouses. If not, take a mental survey of the local bird population and decide which birds nest in houses. Another source of this basic information is your local bird enthusiasts' club or experienced bird hobbyists living near you. Once you have an idea of which species you can expect, you are closer to choosing a design.

As stated above, naturalists have devoted considerable study to birds and their housing requirements. As you can see from Table 7-1 and 7-2, the requirements are very specific for each species. When you consider a commercial house, a design for a homebuilt one, a kit, or your own design, compare its features with those listed to be sure the house will be attractive to the birds you have in mind.

**Table 7-1. Dimension Requirements for Birdhouses. (Source: United States Department of the Interior, "Homes for Birds," Conservation Bulletin 14.)**

| Kind of Bird | A Size of Floor (inches) | B Depth of Bird Box (inches) | C Height of Entrance Above Floor (inches) | D Diameter of Hole (inches) | Height to Fasten Above Ground (feet) |
|---|---|---|---|---|---|
| Bluebird | 5×5 | 8 | 6 | 1 1/2 | 5-10 |
| Chickadee | 4×4 | 8-10 | 6-8 | 1 1/8 | 6-15 |
| Titmouse | 4×4 | 8-10 | 6-8 | 1 1/4 | 6-15 |
| Nuthatch | 4×4 | 8-10 | 6-8 | 1 1/4 | 12-20 |
| House wren and Bewick's wren | 4×4 | 6-8 | 4-6 | 1-1 1/4 | 6-10 |
| Carolina wren | 4×4 | 6-8 | 4-6 | 1 1/2 | 6-10 |
| Violet-green swallow and Tree swallow | 5×5 | 6 | 1-5 | 1 1/2 | 10-15 |
| Purple martin* | 6* | 6* | * | 2 1/2 | 15-20 |
| | UPSb | 2 1/2 | 15-20 | | |
| House finch | 6×6 | 6 | 4 | 2 | 8-12 |
| Starling | 6×6 | 16-18 | 14-16 | 2 | 10-25 |
| Crested flycatcher | 6×6 | 8-10 | 6-8 | 2 | 8-20 |
| Flicker | 7×7 | 16-18 | 14-16 | 2 1/2 | 6-20 |

| | | | | |
|---|---|---|---|---|
| Golden-fronted woodpecker and red-headed wood-pecker | 6×6 | 12-15 | 9-12 | 2 | 12-20 |
| Downy woodpecker | 4×4 | 8-10 | 6-8 | 1 1/4 | 6-20 |
| Hairy woodpecker | 6×6 | 12-15 | 9-12 | 1 1/2 | 12-20 |
| Screech owl | 8×8 | 12-15 | 9-12 | 3 | 10-30 |
| Saw-whet owl | 6×6 | 10-12 | 8-10 | 2 1/2 | 12-20 |
| Barn owl | 10×18 | 15-18 | 4 | 6 | 12-18 |
| Sparrow hawk | 8×8 | 12-15 | 9-12 | 3 | 10-30 |
| Wood duck | 10×18 | 10-24 | 12-16 | 4 | 10-20 |

*b* This and the next table are from *Homes for Birds,* Conservation Bulletin 14, U.S. Department of the Interior, Washington, D.C. For sale by Superintendent of Documents, U.S. Government Printing Office, Washington *25,* D.C.

\* These are dimensions for one compartment, or a martin house for one pair of birds. It is customary to build martin houses eight compartments at a time, which constitutes a section.

When you get around to studying your actual choices, you will quickly see that commercially available birdhouses and kits vary from simply great to absolutely awful. Some have been designed by naturalists or experienced birders. More have just been designed and thrown on the market in an attempt to sell a cute "all-purpose" house. There are dozens of birdhouses on the market. Every discount store, catalog, and nursery sells them. Watch for species-related features and make sure they are built of good quality, durable materials that will stand up to weather. Check to see if their mounting hardware is substantial enough for them to be securely installed. Note features like provisions for adequate ven-

**Table 7-2. Dimension Requirements**
**for Nesting Shelves. (Source: United States Department**
**of the Interior, "Homes for Birds," Conservation Bulletin 14.)**

| Kind of Bird | Size of Floor (inches) | Depth of Bird Box (inches) | Height to Fasten Above Ground (feet) |
|---|---|---|---|
| Robin | 6×8 | 8 | 6-15 |
| Barn swallow | 6×6 | 6 | 8-12 |
| Song sparrow | 6×6 | 6 | 1-3 |
| Phoebe | 6×6 | 6 | 8-12 |

tilation and ease of cleaning. If the commercial house or kit can pass an inspection like this, it probably is a good buy, especially if you have limited building time or interest.

Even when looking for design features other than basic things like size, shape, height above the ground, etc., a little knowledge of your species will help. For example, when deciding whether or not your house should have a perch outside, it is nice to know that wrens and bluebirds do not require perches outside. They are more comfortable flying directly to the entrance. If you do settle on a wren house with a perch, you have probably turned it into a sparrow house because sparrows need and will use perches like these, and they are always looking for a home. As another example, a little reading will tell you that wrens prefer an oval or slot-shaped opening over a round one. Take your time and maybe do a little winter reading while waiting for spring nesting time to come. You will end up with a good, practical house with the right features for what you want to do.

## CONSTRUCTION SPECIFICATIONS

Whether you choose a commercial birdhouse or build your own, there are some basic construction specs that must be met if it is to be durable, weathertight, and attractive to birds and people. You want it used by the birds, after all, and it would be nice if it would last several years. A little attention to the type of materials and construction used will help ensure these things.

### Construction Materials

Wood is by far the best material for building birdhouses. It is easy to cut, sand, and shape, available to everyone, and cheap or even free. In addition, it is a very poor conductor of heat, acting like a natural insulator, so it stays relatively cool in the summer. Imagine a birdhouse of metal or even plastic in the summer. They really get hot—in fact, sometimes hot enough to kill fledglings inside. You will also find that wood will not get brittle and warp nearly as badly as most plastics. Another advantage is that wood can be either glued or fastened with nails or screws, while plastics generally are not so versatile. Finally, because wood is a natural material for birds, it is most attractive to them. I suggest that even if you are not going to build your own birdhouse, you should look for a commercial one or a kit built of wood.

When you start looking for wood to build with, you will probably look around the garage first. None of us likes to go out and spend money if we can make do with something laying around the house. Just look for good quality wood even though it may be weathered and aged. I like weathered wood for building because it gives the structure a natural look. Pine and cedar are both good, but my personal preference is for cypress fencing boards. Cypress, like cedar, resists rot and weather damage for years. Fence boards with their rough sawn texture are excellent for houses. If you don't have any extras from your fence, they are available at any fencing dealer for 2 to 3 dollars for a 3/8-inch-thick, 6-inch-wide-by-6-foot-long board. One board will build most types of houses. They are also available in 1/4-inch thickness, and they will work well, too, but I like the extra thickness to nail or screw into.

The inside of your birdhouse should be left rough, so plan your building materials accordingly. This interior roughness is important as birds must be able to get a purchase on the insides of the house to be able to scramble up to the entrance hole. If you must use smooth planed wood, you can rough up the insides of the boards before assembly with a drill or hobby grinder. The cypress fencing is, of course, a good choice for building a natural rough interior. Another good choice is to use what is called slab stock or outside cuts. These are the first boards that are cut off the trimmed log at the sawmill, and they still have bark on the side. If you have a local sawmill or lumber yard that stocks outside cuts, they are super for birdhouses. You can build your house with the bark side in and have a nearly natural interior surface.

Many of us have scraps of plywood around the workshop, and this can be another good building material. It is easy to work with and comes in many thicknesses. My cautions are with the difficulty about nailing or screwing into the ends of very thin plywood. Not only is it critical to line up and nail or drill, but there is a tendency for it to split between plys. Thicker plywood is more workable when it comes to end nailing or screwing. In addition, you should be a little careful about building birdhouses out of interior-grade plywood and then exposing them to years of rain and storms outside. Interior plys aren't manufactured with glues as waterproof as exterior-grade plywood is. If you use interior-grade ply, be sure to give it a minimum of two coats of varnish or other good sealer. I do not recommend using particle board or pegboard at all because I have never been able to waterproof them enough to have them last more than a year.

### Hardware, Adhesives, and Fasteners

Because you want your birdhouse to look nice and last for several seasons, it makes sense to be sure it is built with quality hardware that will not rust and fall apart, good adhesives that will not crack or fail, and fasteners that will not rust and come loose. It only takes a fractional increase in the building cost to include these quality items, and it sure pays off in the end.

When I talk about hardware for birdhouses, I mean hinges, eyebolts for hanging, hooks and eyes or latches, and so forth. Most designs are at least going to have a hinge or two to enable you to open it up for easy cleaning. Look for hinges that appear strong enough to stand up to years of use instead of attractive little decorative ones. Hooks and other hanging hardware should be designed without pieces that might rust and weaken or bend in a windstorm. In general, brass hardware will last longer with less corrosion and little or no rust. Your hardware store will have a very large selection of hardware and people to give you good advice.

Over the past few years, there has been an absolute explosion in the variety of different adhesives available. There are new "super" glues, two-part epoxies, and silicone adhesives that make building a snap. Carpenter's white glue is still very good for joining wood, especially if the glue joint is also to be nailed or screwed, but let's take a closer look at the newcomers.

Instant *cyanoacrylate* "super" glues are handy for tacking pieces together or for permanent bonding of tight-fitting joints. These glues are water thin and do not fill gaps very well. Unless your pieces are absolutely flush against each other, they will not bond well. The exception to this is if you fill the gap you want to bond with common baking soda and then drop on the "super" glue. There will be an instant chemical reaction and the baking soda will turn rock hard, filling the gap. Cyanoacrylates are totally waterproof and last for years. They do tend to be relatively expensive, especially for large projects. You can, however, assemble an entire birdhouse with one of the "super" glues and baking soda in a few minutes with absolutely no clamping, nails or screws, or even waiting for the glue to set.

The two-part epoxy glues are really great, too. They come in quick-cure types that set and cure in only 6 to 10 minutes and in slower-cure types that take up to 3 hours to set. Epoxies are extremely strong and versatile adhesives. With the quick-cure types you can actually glue one joint, hold it secure with your hands for four or five minutes while it cures, and then go on to the next one.

Like the cyanoacrylates, the epoxies make it possible to assemble an entire birdhouse in just about no time. The drawback to them is that they are relatively expensive, too, though less so than the "super" glues. You will find, however, that once you use either of them you will probably become a convert. Epoxies are totally waterproof and will last for many years.

As a final note, I have been experimenting with the use of silicone sealant as an adhesive for birdhouse construction, and it has been working out great. Silicone sealant is the stuff marketed by that name and also under the name of "bathtub caulk" or "silicone adhesive." It is thick enough to fill any gaps or irregularities in your glue joints, sets within a couple of hours, and cures totally overnight. It is less expensive than epoxy. Because it is slower to set, it causes you to have a clamp or otherwise secure your work. Silicone remains flexible for years, which means it take temperature change well and allows for the shrinkage and flexing of wood in different seasons. It is also nontoxic to birds and other animals. I have two houses that were assembled using only silicone adhesive set out on a bluebird trail. This is the houses' second season outdoors, and I am pleased with how they are holding up.

Most of us are more familiar with joining wood with nails or screws than with the new adhesives. There is something strong and secure about a screwed or nailed joint. If you decide to use fasteners like this, you will find that, like better quality hardware, brass screws and galvanized nails make up for their extra expense by giving longer service. The appearance of your birdhouse will stay much more attractive without rusty nailheads and screws. Be sure, too, that you select the proper size fastener. Using nails too short or too thin will cause them to fail to hold as well as they should, and as years go by with seasonal flexing, shrinking, and swelling of the wood, they will work their way out. On the other hand, trying to nail into the end of a piece of wood with a too large diameter nail is bound to cause a serious split. I like to choose a nail about twice as long as the thickness of wood I am using. In other words, to join two 3/8-inch cypress birdhouse sides, I will use a 3/4-inch nail. This is just a rule of thumb, however. Any size in the ballpark will do.

If you use screws to fasten your house together, the same rules apply about choosing a size that is large enough to hold securely and yet small enough so that it won't split the board. When you get ready to put in a screw, always drill a pilot hole first. The hole should be a size or two smaller than the size screw you have. This will help you keep your pieces lined up, make screwing in the screw easier, and avoid most cases of split end pieces. In general, I prefer screws over nails because they show less tendency to work their way out over the years and can be tightened from time to time.

## Special Design Requirements

No matter what type of birdhouse you finally settle on, there are a few design requirements that will ensure it is a comfortable, healthy home for birds. Naturally, you should be sure it is weather-tight and well constructed, but there are other considerations, too.

Adequate ventilation is very important in a birdhouse. Baby birds left helpless during the day in a house in direct sunlight often die from overheating. Even the thickest wood will not keep the temperatures low enough if no provision has been made for good ventilation. Look at your birdhouse or design. There should be ventilation holes bored around the top of the walls, under the roof overhang, so rain will not drip in. If your commercial house or your design does not include ventilation holes drill 3/8-inch holes all around. It is especially nice to bore the holes at an upward angle as further insurance against rain running in. Ventilation holes are important in any house, but especially in plastic ones as they tend to get hotter than wooden ones.

Another hazard for baby birds is, believe it or not, drowning. During severe rains sometimes quite a lot of water will get into a birdhouse. If you don't have drain holes in the bottom, it will accumulate and, at best, make the occupants very uncomfortable. Once again, no matter what type of birdhouse you have, look at the bottom and be sure it has drain holes. If it doesn't, drill a few 1/4-inch holes at random across the bottom. You should drill more than one or two as they tend to become clogged with nesting materials and waste. Drain holes not only allow excess moisture to pass out of the birdhouse, but they also increase ventilation, acting to give more of a "flow-through" effect.

The third design requirement is for some means of opening the house up for easy cleaning. This is very often overlooked. If your house is to be up more than a single season, it will have to be cleaned. There should be some simple way of inserting a brush and giving it a good scrubbing out. Most homebuilt birdhouses have either hinged roofs or bottoms. Either is fine as they give you a large opening. It is the commercial houses you have to watch. Many of the ones I have seen give you no convenient way of cleaning them at all. If you have one like this, it is pretty hard to remedy. I suggest buying or building a new one that is a better design.

## Painting and Finishing

After you buy or assemble your birdhouse, it is only natural that you want it to look its best when you put it up for the birds to begin using. The trouble is, what looks best to many of us is not necessarily what looks most attractive to nesting birds. You might love bright yellow birdhouses with green shutters, but remember that we are trying to get birds to nest inside, and to be most successful, we have to try and simulate a natural nesting place as much as possible.

From the bird's standpoint, the most attractive house is natural, rustic brown, grey, or dark green, with a rough-sawn or even a bark-covered exterior. Although many of our common yard birds are so used to mankind by now that they will nest about anywhere, bright colors and shiny finishes still will not encourage as many birds as will a weathered-looking natural color.

When I build a birdhouse, I often don't use any stain or paint at all if I use cypress or redwood. I just leave them up to weather to a nice natural shade of grey-brown. If you are not satisfied with the natural color of your wood, you might want to apply a coat or two of stain. This will keep the original texture of the wood and still give a natural color, too. Varnish adds waterproofing and durability in severe climates or to woods like plywood that are not naturally long lasting. Paint will add durability, but it should not be too bright a color. If your birdhouse is to be in a very sunny area, you will want to stay with a lighter color. White, in general, is not a great color for birdhouses, because it is a bright, high-contrast color, but for martin houses, which are out in the direct sunlight, it is a necessity.

If you use paint, stain, or varnish on your birdhouse, don't plan on putting it up for birds' use for two to three weeks. It takes that long for all the paint and thinner fumes to dissipate. If you put it out too soon after painting, the fumes might drive prospective nesters away or harm baby birds. If you have the benefit of enough time to plan ahead, you might be able to prepare and hang your birdhouses in the winter. This will give them several weeks for the paint fumes to dissipate, for the house to acquire a rustic, natural appearance and scent, and for prospective nesters to look it over and get used to it. The same thing goes for refurbishing old houses.

Take them down and redo them in the fall when you do your bird-house cleaning. Rehang them in the winter, and you will ensure that they have time to air out and weather a bit before the spring nesters get ready to use them.

## LOCATING AND INSTALLING YOUR BIRDHOUSE

Because you are going to the trouble and expense of providing birdhouses for the birds in your yard, you certainly hope they will be used. It is always a disappointment to have them sit empty day after day after you were so expectant. We have all had it happen. Sometimes the most proven design in the most bird-filled yard will go unused for years. Often I have turned them into popular nesting sites simply by moving them to another spot in the yard or installing them in a different manner. Because of this, choosing a good location for and installing your birdhouses deserves a closer look.

### Location

The key to choosing a location for your birdhouse is to try and find a spot as near to where the bird would naturally nest as possible. Refer again to the table on birdhouse specifications to see how high above the ground these common birds prefer to nest. That will set a height for you. A little more research will tell you if that particular type of bird prefers an open setting or dense foliage. Because the house will be used for spring and summer nesting, consider your climate and factor on whether the house will be too hot out in full sun. If so, opt for partial shading. About the only birds for whom I recommend a house in full sun are martins. For the rest, a partially shaded, or even mostly shaded (but not dark) area is best if you live in a very hot part of the country.

As you can see, we are trying to find a comfortable, natural setting for the house. We also need to place it where birds will feel secure and safe. For shy birds it might be necessary to place the house in a more secluded part of your yard away from your house. If you live in an area with many wandering cats, you will want to place the house where there are few bushes and other hiding places. This will cut down the chances of having your nesting birds ambushed.

Nesting birds are territorial and will squabble fiercely over nesting sites and territory. A general rule is to avoid placing more than one house per species per yard unless your yard is very large. For placing birdhouses of different species, try to place them at least 30 feet apart and with a height difference of 6 to 10 feet if possible. This will help promote harmony. I have had warring families of mockingbirds in my yards now for several seasons, and it can get very noisy and raucous at times.

## Installation

Once you have chosen a suitable location for the birdhouse, it is time to install it. You will want to take a look at the mounting hardware and the way the instructions or plans suggest to mount the house to be sure that it is a sturdy method and that you understand it fully. If you are not satisfied, look at the following birdhouse plans and at the ways feeders were mounted in Chapter 6. Try to adapt one of the mounting methods to your circumstances. This is especially important for commercial houses because their mounting methods are often too weak to last several seasons.

Birdhouses that are meant to be mounted against a tree trunk, house, fence, or other upright surface are usually fitted with extensions either on the sides or top and bottom to screw through

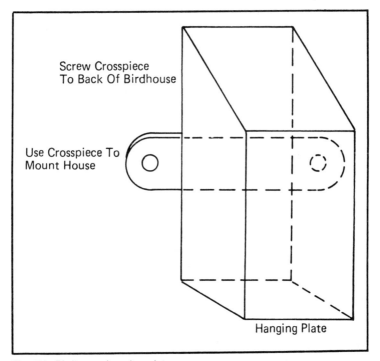

Fig. 7-1. Birdhouse hanging plate.

and into the mounting surface. If your birdhouse is not fitted out like that, I suggest that you modify it. Trying to screw through the inside back of the house or depending on holes to hook over nails sticking out of the upright surface will not serve well for long. It is simpler and longer lasting if you make a hanging plate out of thin wood as wide as the back of the birdhouse plus 4 inches, center it on the back of the house, and screw it on securely. As you can see in Fig. 7-1, your house has 2-inch extensions on either side. These extensions are just right to drill and screw through into the wall or fence. For mounting on trees, you can drill larger holes in the extensions and run rope or cord around the tree to tie it on without damage to the tree. Hanging plates like this can also be made to extend up and down the height of the birdhouse if that is more appropriate to your mounting needs. Large angle brackets offer another way to mount houses against upright surfaces.

If your house is designed to be pole mounted, I suggest mounting it the same way you would a pole-mounted feeder. Use a pipe flange arrangement or angle brackets. Glance back at the suggestions in Chapter 6 for specifics. As with feeders, I prefer using smooth metal pipe for mounting rather than wooden posts because cats and squirrels can climb wooden posts so easily. If you do end up using the posts, it is easy to make a circular cat and squirrel cone to deter these clever climbers. There are plans for one in Chapter 6.

Whichever type of pole you end up with, it is important to refer back to Table 7-1 for the proper height to place birdhouses for each variety of bird. This will help you select a proper height for your pole. Keep it on the long side, however, to minimize cat and squirrel trouble. Finally, be certain you can take the house down fairly easily for seasonal cleaning and upkeep.

Martin houses present special problems since they are mounted so high. Most of them are positioned too high to reach with a common ladder, so you must have some means of lowering them for cleaning and repairs. One way of doing it is shown in Fig. 7-2. As you can see, the actual mounting pipe is set tightly into a piece of wood. This piece of wood fits between two others that have been bedded firmly in concrete. The three are joined using two large bolts running all the way through them. When it is time to lower the house, one of the bolts is removed, allowing the middle block of wood and the pipe and house to pivot down. For actually mounting the house to the pipe, the standard pipe flange system is good. However you finally decide to mount it, bear in mind that it will

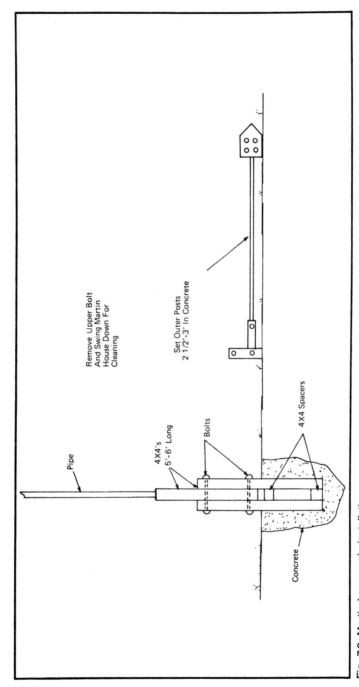

Remove Upper Bolt
And Swing Martin
House Down For
Cleaning

Set Outer Posts
2 1/2'-3' In Concrete

Pipe

4X4's
5'-6' Long

Bolts

4X4 Spacers

Concrete

Fig. 7-2. Martin house pole installation.

113

be subject to high storm winds, and a large house like that break-ing loose could mean property damage and danger to humans as well as birds.

## CLEANING AND MAINTENANCE

Like just about anything else I can think of, keeping your birdhouses in top-top shape involves a little work. I like to look at these chores as evidence that the houses are popular and used. After all, if no birds ever used them they would never have to be cleaned, repaired, or modified. The work involved only amounts to a cou-ple of hours a year, and that isn't much compared to the hours of enjoyment you will have from busy nesters using them.

After every nesting season, it is important to clean the houses and remove all the waste and old nesting materials. If you leave all that refuse inside the house, you are inviting parasites and creating an unattractive nesting site. Many people like to take down their houses immediately after the end of the nesting season and give them a good cleaning. Then they either store them away until late winter or put them back up. If they put them back up, they have to decide whether or not they are going to leave them open to allow birds to shelter in them over the winter. Leaving them open means that the houses will have to be cleaned again before nesting begins. Houses that will not be open for shelter will have their openings plugged or covered over until early spring. Another ap-proach is to leave the cleaning chore until late winter. Then, whether birds have been allowed to shelter inside or not, a thorough scrubbing will make the house spic and span for nesting. Whether you are a summer cleaner or a late winter cleaner doesn't really matter. Just be sure to get the houses clean and ready by early spring.

The actual job of cleaning will be a snap if your house is de-signed for it. If it has a large roof or bottom that hinges open, all you have to do is dismount the house, open it, use a stick or similar tool to clear out the nesting materials, and then give the inside a scouring with a wire brush. As a final step scrub the inside with your brush and hot water and detergent. Leave it open in the sun to dry for several days before you replace it. I find that this hot water and soap scrubbing is usually all it takes unless there are obvious parasites in the old nesting material. If there are, clearing it out removes most of them, the scrubbing even more, and then a dusting with pesticide takes care of the remainder. If you have to use a pesticide, be sure to choose one especially formulated to work against bird parasites. Let the house sit and air out several weeks before you allow any bird to nest in it.

Almost all birdhouse maintenance is done during your seasonal cleaning. Check to be sure the drain holes on the bottom are open and free from obstructions. If they re not, redrill them as needed. Check the glue joints, nails, screws, hinges, and other hardware on the house itself and make necessary repairs. Be certain to pay special attention to the mounting of the house because it takes a lot of stress being pushed and swayed about in the wind day after day.

From time to time you might want to do more to your birdhouses than standard cleaning and maintenance requires. If boards have warped or twisted, making the birdhouse unsightly or no longer weatherproof, you can replace them without rebuilding the entire house. I tend to prefer filling the cracks with silicone sealer and letting the birdhouse look warped and weathered. Sometimes entry holes get gnawn larger by birds or squirrels and need refacing. It is easy to reface them by cutting a fake front for the part of the birdhouse around the opening from thin wood, or for more permanence, thin metal. Cut a properly sized opening in this facade and glue or nail it on over the existing entry hole. I have one old house that has been refaced like this three times. It has rather thick front now, but it is still giving good service. You might be happier with a new coat of paint from time to time, too. For these types of major overhauls follow the same construction guidelines as in initial building when it comes to materials and letting it set long enough before occupancy for paint, glue, and other fumes to totally dissipate.

## UNWANTED TENANTS

Two main categories of unwanted tenants will try to occupy your birdhouses—winter guests and varieties of birds you would rather not have nest there. At some time you are bound to have a problem with one or the other category. It is surprising how exasperatingly persistent some of these problem visitors can be. I have even known people who have abandoned their birdhouses after loosing the battles and the war against them.

Winter guests are not unwanted tenants to many bird lovers. They consider their birdhouses winter shelter and accept the fact that the houses are going to get a little more wear and tear and a lot more dirty because of it. In severe climates, birds will often crowd into houses on cold nights until there literally isn't room for any more to enter. In fact, one winter morning as the sun warmed up a house in my yard I watched four sparrows emerge. Normally they would squabble and sqawk crowded together like that, but in the winter survival comes first. Squirrels also love to winter in birdhouses because they are not unlike their natural tree holes in shape.

There are problems with allowing your houses to be used as winter shelter even aside from the obvious one of dirt and droppings accumulating in them. Wintering birds and squirrels especially will often gnaw the openings larger to make it easier to come and go. As you will remember from the design specifications chart, entry hole size is a critical factor in attracting nesting birds. Smaller entry holes keep out larger, more aggressive birds that would soon take over the nest site. Therefore, if wintering birds and squirrels enlarge the entry holes, your birdhouses might end up as homes for different species than you had in mind. You may also find that the birds who wintered in your birdhouse might not feel like moving on come spring. Sometimes you can scare the same tenacious bird out of a house a dozen times, and he will keep coming back. By the time your desired species arrives to look for a nesting site, your winter friend is firmly entrenched.

Winter guests can be kept out by plugging the entry holes on your houses with rags, corks, wooden plugs, etc., or by attaching a little wooden disk over the entry by one nail or screw so that it can be swung down over the entry hole. You can even simply tape over the entry holes with duct tape.

Trying to keep unwanted species from nesting in your birdhouses is a tough problem. Sparrows and wrens will nest about anywhere and are aggressive enough to take a house away from most songbirds. The best way to keep out birds you don't want is by design features. For example, place the house at a height and location that are unattractive to them. Make sure the opening size is right for your desired birds and wrong for others. Sparrows must have outside perches to be able to use a house comfortably, so try to choose a design that does not have any unless perches are necessary for your desired species. In my experience, all these things help but never work 100 percent of the time. Very often some terribly insistent bird will ignore my precautions and my attempts to frighten it off and set up housekeeping in a house I had reserved for a totally different species. Once the eggs are laid, I give up and hope for better luck next year.

## MAKING A BIRDHOUSE USING
## A CARDBOARD BOX AS A FORM

For inexperienced builders, putting together all the right angles to build a square, well-fitting birdhouse can be tough. Even with all the parts measured and cut out correctly, if you aren't careful, you can end up with a crooked structure that roof and bottom pieces will not fit. One way I have found to ensure that beginners have a good chance at success is to have them use a stout cardboard box as an inner form. The box helps shape the house during assembly by keeping it from shifting into a lopsided parallelogram instead of a square or rectangle. Once it has done its job, it is pulled out and discarded, leaving a good frame behind.

The materials list for a house to be built over a form is short and easy. Naturally you will need a sturdy cardboard box of the proper size. It cannot be one of the thin types. These just cave in during the assembly of the house. Find one that is designed for shipping or to protect fragile items. The best ones are of corregated cardboard, about 3/16 of an inch thick. To determine the size box you need, scan the chart on birdhouse dimensions. Find which birds are likely to visit your yard, and then read the size requirements for those birds. You are likely to have a box around the house that fits the inner floor dimensions just right. It does not matter if the box is too tall, but it must be as tall as the recommended height of the house. The wood for a house like this should be thin, 1/4-inch plywood or 3/8-inch redwood, cedar, or cypress fencing board. The exact amount depends, of course, on the size of house you are building. The other items needed are a tube of silicone sealant (bathtub caulk works fine, and it comes in several colors including clear), several large, strong rubber bands, some 3/4- to 1-inch nails or tacks and two 1- to 1 1/2-inch nails.

To begin, use the chart to decide on the proper height for the house you are building. Cut the cardboard box off at that height. Take a marker and mark the four upright sides of your box "front," "back," "side 1," and "side 2." Lay the "front" against your wood stock and carefully trace around it. Be sure you trace close to the side of the box. Go ahead and cut out this piece and sand its edges smooth. Measure up the center of it to the height recommended in the chart for the entrance opening and make a heavy mark there. Refer again to the chart for the proper entrance size, and, using the mark you made as the center, draw the entrance hole. Drill a starter hole with a drill, insert a coping saw, and cut out the entrance hole. Next lay the box side marked "back" against the wood, trace around it, and cut it out. Take some medium grit sandpaper and sand both pieces smooth. Then lay them aside.

To cut out the sides, lay each one against the wood and trace around it. Then, in addition to marking each piece "side 1" and "side 2," also mark "top" and "bottom" on each. To each of these side pieces you must add enough width to allow it to overlap the front and back pieces. To decide how much to add to the width, measure the thickness of your wood and double it. That means if you are using 1/4-inch plywood, you will add 1/2 inch to the width of each side piece. Be sure you don't add it to the top or bottom. You must add it to the width. Once you have the extra added, go ahead and cut out the two side pieces and give them a quick sanding.

To make the roof and bottom pieces, trace the bottom of the box twice. Then, decide which one you want to be the roof and enlarge it by adding 1 inch to each of the two sides and to what will be the front edge of the roof. This extra size will allow for the roof overhang. Cut these two pieces out and sand them, too.

To begin the actual assembly, run a thick bead of silicone adhesive along the side edges of the back piece. Put it in place against the back of the box. Fit the two side pieces against it so that they overlap the back piece and fit well against the sides of the box. Use several strong rubber bands to hold the structure together while it dries—at least overnight.

Once you have made sure the silicone adhesive is dry, it is time to remove the box-form. Since the box is bound to have stuck to the corners, you will need to trim it away with a sharp knife. To do this, first cut out the box-bottom, then simply cut loose each corner by slicing the cardboard on either side, about 1/2 inch away. I don't trim any more cardboard away because the birds peck and shread it and use it for nesting material.

Now you should be left with a three-sided box. Take the bottom piece, run adhesive around the back and side edges, and slide it into place. It will help to keep the box square. Turn the box on its side and tap in a couple of thin nails on each side to keep it in place while you work on the front.

Fit the front piece into position between the two sides. Measure halfway down the sides, along the edge where the side piece overlaps the front piece, and make a mark. Do the same for the other side. This is where you will place the pivot nails that will allow you to swing the front piece open for cleaning. Once you are sure that these marks are in the same relative position on each side, nail the pivot nails into place. Do not use any glue or other fastenings on the front piece.

All that remains is to attach the roof. For this you simply run a good bead of silicone sealant around top edges of the back and side pieces and seat it in place. Be sure to notice that you should have 1 inch of overhang on each side and in the front, but *none* in the back. If you attach the roof so that there is an overhang in the back you will not be able to mount the house flush against anything. Once you have it on properly, place a book or two in it to weight it down and let it dry overnight.

Once your basic structure is complete and dry, the finishing touches don't take very long. Use a 1/4-inch drill to drill several ventilation holes up under the roof overhang. Make them close to the roof to protect them from rain as much as possible. Drill several drainage and ventilation holes in the bottom, too. Pivot the door open and look at the silicone sealing the roof to the house. If necessary, run another bead along the seam to further seal it. Don't worry about having exposed sealant inside because it is nontoxic and won't hurt birds if they nip at it. Check the outer seams, too, and use a knife to trim off any extra silicone that is protruding.

Weatherproofing the wood is the next step. If you use cedar, cypress, or redwood fencing board or siding, you don't have to do anything at all. These woods last years in the weather. Other woods, especially plywood or other composite woods, need serious protection if they are to last more than a year. If you are not satisfied with the original wood color, I recommend natural stains and at least two coats of varnish. If you prefer paint, choose an earthy color. Try to avoid bright colors because they are unattractive to birds used to nesting among browns and greens. If you must place the house where it will be in the sun, use white because it is the coolest color. To fully weatherproof your house, use at least two coats of paint. By the way, you will find that most of the silicone sealants on the market take stain or paint very well.

To hang this style of birdhouse you can simply pivot open the front and screw through the back of the house directly into a tree or post. If you would rather not use this method or if you simply want to protect your tree, there are two other methods to consider. First, you can drill two holes through the back of the house, thread in some strong cord, lace it through and out again, and tie the house in place. The other method is to cut a piece of scrap wood about 3 inches wide and as long as the house is tall plus 6 inches. Lay the open house on this hanging strip, center it, and drill and screw through the back of the house into it. Then you can use the hanging strip to nail through or drill and lace cord through for tying the house in place.

## NUTHATCH, TITMOUSE, OR CHICKADEE HOUSE

Because the house dimension requirements for all three of these

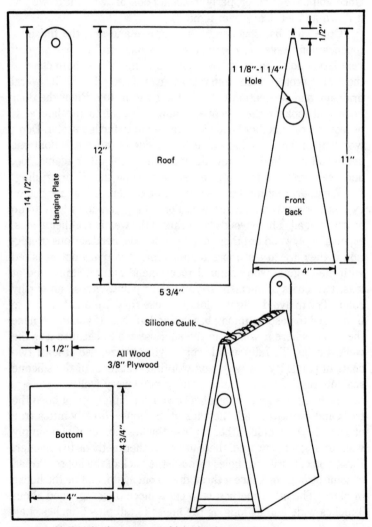

Fig. 7-3. Nuthatch, titmouse, or chickadee house plan.

- 3/8-inch plywood.
- Silicone bathtub caulk-type adhesive.
- 3/4-inch or 1-inch nails or small screws (minimum of 30).
- 2 small hinges.
- 2 small hooks and eyes or other fasteners.
- Paint or other finish as desired.

Fig. 7-4. Materials list for the nuthatch, titmouse, or chickadee house.

types of birds are about the same except for the size of the entrance opening and the height at which you install it, with very minor changes, this design will do triple duty for you. As you can see from Fig. 7-3, it is an easy house for a beginner to build. Being small and basic in shape, it nestles in the foliage and assumes a natural look that many birds prefer over brighter, more ornate houses. Although it may look like you need to cut and fit special angles and bevel edges to make them fit, it is not so. All the angles come automatically as you measure, draw out, and join the individual pieces.

Begin by checking the materials list for this project (Fig. 7-4). Then draw out each piece you will need on your plywood. First draw out the front and back. Do both at the same time by carefully measuring and sketching out a rectangle 4 inches wide by 22 inches tall. Mark a centerline up and down the rectangle. Mark another centerline across it at 11 inches. Lay a long straightedge from corner to corner diagonally across. Being careful that you are passing through the point where the two centerlines intersect. Repeat with the other diagonal corners. You will end up with two triangles with 4-inch bases and 11-inch heights, just what you need for the front and back. Cut them out and lay one aside. On the other one, measure up 7 inches along the centerline and make a mark. This will be the center of the entrance hole. Use a compass to mark a 1 1/4 circle (1 1/8-inch circle for chickadees) around this mark. If a compass isn't handy, find any round shape of the proper size to trace. For my latest version of this house, I found that the cap from a bottle of rubbing alcohol was perfect. If you scout around the house, you will find something suitable. Once you have the entrance marked, use a coping saw or jigsaw to cut it out. As a last step, cut 1/2 inch off the point at the top of the triangle. This will make a well protected vent hole up under the overhang. Lay the front aside.

Next you will cut out the two roof pieces. Because you need a small overhang in front to shelter the entrance, the roof pieces are slightly wider than the actual width of the house. Measure and mark a line 1 inch in from the edge along what will be the inside front of each roof piece. These lines will help you position the roof when it is time to attach it. This line-up is important if the bottom is to fit properly.

All you have left to cut out are the bottom and the hanging plate. When you cut out the bottom piece, drill several 1/4-inch drain holes in it. The hanging plate is attached to the birdhouse so that you have its extensions on top and bottom to use when you nail or tie the unit to a tree or post. After you have all the pieces cut out, give each one a quick touch with sandpaper. You are ready to begin the actual assembly.

Lay the back of the house on edge and trail fit one of the roof pieces to it. Be sure you are not using the side of the roof where you marked the 1-inch overhang line. After you get these two pieces lined up carefully, apply adhesive if you are using it, and nail or screw through the roof piece and into the back. Attach the other roof piece the same way, butting them together at the roof peak as closely as possible. Note that the roof pieces overhang the bottom of the front and back pieces. Do not attempt to nail or screw into the peak, and do not be concerned if they don't meet in a perfect fit. Take the silicone caulk and squeeze a neat bead along the peak joint on the inside of the house. Then do the same on the outside, being careful to get a neat, smooth fill of the area between the two roof sections.

The next step is one that is easy to forget because you tend to feel that you should go ahead and put the front on now. Not so. Next is the hanging plate. Lay the birdhouse on it and center it top to bottom and side to side. Nail or screw through the back of the house and into the plate. Attach it securely because this is the only support for the weight of the house. Now get the house front and trail fit it. Slide it in place being careful to line it up on the inside overhang lines so the overhang will be built in. When you are satisfied with the fit, lay the house on its side, apply glue to the edges of the front, and nail or screw through the roof pieces and into the front of the house.

The floor of this house simply butts up against the bottom instead of being inset. As you trial fit the bottom to the house, you will see that you will hinge between the bottom and the back of the house. Install the hinges, close the bottom snugly, and fasten it shut using small hooks and eyes, a cabinet latch, or some small wire loops to slip over tacks or screws. Using two fasteners will help keep the bottom from warping out of shape and also give you a margin of safety in case one fails.

Because this house is built of plywood, I recommend some sort of weatherproofing for the wood. You may like paint, stain and varnish, or plain varnish. However you weatherproof it, be sure to remember to wait a couple of weeks for all the finish materials to outgas before you put the house up for occupancy. Then, find a good spot, 12 to 20 feet from the ground for nuthatches or 6 to 15 feet above the ground for chickadees and titmice, and install it. I have had the best luck placing houses for these birds in tall pine trees where I use light nylon cord to tie them securely rather than nailing into the tree. Tying also makes the houses easier to take down each year for cleaning.

## FLICKER HOUSE

Flickers are such large birds that a flicker house is the largest single-birdhouse in the book. This tends to make them simple to build because the pieces are large and easy to handle. By the way, this plan can be modified to accommodate any woodpecker. Simply look at the chart on birdhouse dimensions (Table 7-1) and change the measurements accordingly.

Study the plan for this house (Fig. 7-5) and the materials list (Fig. 7-6). Then lay out the dimensions on your wood. Be careful to measure and mark accurately and use a square to ensure even corners. Cut out and back and front shapes, and then measure up the center of the front piece to 14 inches from the bottom. Make a mark here that will be the center of the 2 1/2-inch entrance hole. Use a compass or proper sized round pattern to draw the entrance hole. Then drill a starter hole for a saw blade and cut out the hole. Cut out the two sides and the roof. When you cut out the bottom piece, go ahead and drill several 1/4-inch drain holes in it. This will save a step later on. Lightly sand all the pieces, and set them aside.

To begin construction, stand one of the side pieces on its back edge and nail or screw the front to it. If you are using adhesive along with fasteners, run a bead of it along each joint before you secure it. Next, attach the front to the other side piece the same way. Note that the sides fit *inside* the front and back instead of overlapping them. The next step is to lay the house front down and position the back piece. Notice that there is no overlap at the bot-

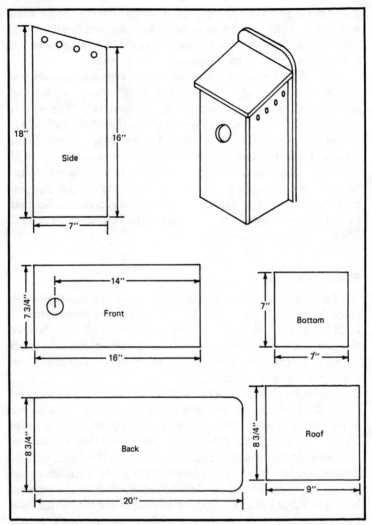

Fig. 7-5. Plan for the flicker house.

tom of the house, but be sure to allow for the 1/2-inch overlap on each side. Glue and nail or screw the back in place. Fit the bottom now. This is often tricky because unless you are very careful your birdhouse will not be exactly square. Plan on having to sand and trim the bottom to make it fit up inside the bottom of the house. If you have gaps, it really does not matter too much because they only increase your drainage and ventilations. The gaps can, however, easily be filled with silicone sealant. Attach the bottom securely, and your flicker house is nearly finished.

Your next step is to trial fit the roof piece. Then use two hinges to attach the roof to the back of the birdhouse. Hinging the top of a birdhouse can allow water to seep in, but we get around that problem through the use of silicone sealant, too. Simply open the roof wide, and run a good bead of sealant along the gap on the house side rather than the roof side. Try not to get any on the hinges. Then cover the sealant with a small piece of plastic wrap to prevent it from sticking to the roof. Close the roof and fasten it down snugly. The sealant will be pressed into the gap forming a nice, gasketlike seal. Allow it to dry and cure. Then open the roof and trim any excess sealant with a razor blade. Add whatever type of fasteners you prefer, hooks and eyes or whatever, and all that remains is to drill vent holes up under the overhang. Drill them at a slight upward angle to keep rain from dripping in. Paint or finish the house as you desire. Keep in mind that birds want as natural-looking a house as possible. Mount the house securely in a spot between 6 and 20 feet off the ground.

---

- 3/8-inch plywood.
- Adhesive or glue for joining sides (optional).
- 3/4-inch or 1-inch finishing nails or small screws (minimum of 30).
- Silicone bathtub caulktype adhesive.
- 2 hooks and eyes or similar fasteners.
- Paint, varnish, or other finish as desired.

---

Fig. 7-6. List of materials for the flicker house.

## CHICKADEE LOG CABIN

This rustic-looking birdhouse is fun to build and as natural a nesting site as you can build for hole nesting birds. As you can see from Fig. 7-7, the only materials needed are a log, some wood screws, and the means for hanging it, so it is a bargain, too.

The first step in this project is to find a suitable log to work with. If you live in a rural or woodsy suburban area, you can probably find a limb from a downed tree. One of the easiest sources of good, seasoned logs is a shop that sells firewood. You can pick and choose from already cut logs and take one home for very little money. Choose one a minimum of 6 inches across and 12 to 15

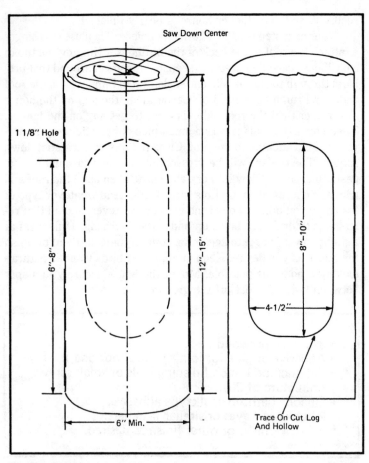

Fig. 7-7. Chickadee log cabin plan.

inches long. It should be as straight as possible and fairly free of bumps, knots, etc. Trim it as necessary to remove jagged edges and loose bark, and you are ready to build.

Mark a centerline all the way up the side of the log as straight as possible, and saw it in half lengthwise. A bandsaw or radial arm saw works very well. Lay out the two halves, cut side up, and line them up side by side. Mark the areas to be cut out. The hollow will be 8 to 10 inches deep and be about 4 1/2 inches across. The easiest way I have found to mark it is to draw out these dimensions on scrap paper and then cut this pattern out, lay it over the cut surface of the log, and trace around it. Then do the same with the other half log, lining them up so the traced areas are in the same relative position on the two logs. This eliminates a lot of measuring. From here it is simply a matter of digging out the hollow. I use a sharp wood chisel and a hammer to remove the wood inside my traced lines until the two halves have mostly rounded hollows of the proper depth of around 2 1/4 inches. You could also use a hobby grinder to burr out the unwanted wood. When finished, your house should have the proper 8- to 10-inch depth and a roughly cylindrical hollow with a circumference of about 4 1/2 inches. Leave the inside naturally rough.

Trial fit the two halves of the log back together, and then choose one to be the front of the house. On this one, measure 6 to 8 inches from the floor of the house (not from the bottom of the log) and bore a 1 1/8-inch entrance hole. Fit the two halves back together and secure them tightly with several rubber bands or tape. Drill pilot holes for two long wood screws at the top of the house and two at the bottom to hold the house together and to let you open it for yearly cleaning.

There are several ways to mount a log house. You can simply wire or tie it on, or you can nail or screw through the back of the house into the tree or post. With the round surface of the log, these are not always the best methods, so let's look at alternatives. If your log is thick enough, you can carefully saw off some of the back of the house to create a flat area to rest against the mounting surface. Then you can go ahead and mount it directly or make and use a hanging plate like the one used on the nuthatch house. You can also use angle brackets to mount this house, just be sure the ends of the log are fairly straight. Then attach angle brackets to the top and bottom for mounting to the tree or post. Locate the house in a protected area 6 to 15 feet above the ground.

## WOODPECKER HOUSE

This basic design house (Fig. 7-8) has the correct dimensions for golden-fronted, hairy, and red-headed woodpeckers. As we did for the nuthatch/chickadee/titmouse house, we will merely have to change the size of the entrance hole to optimize it to a certain species. In addition, a look at the birdhouse dimensions chart will show you that it would be very simple to change the measurements slightly and turn it into a downy woodpecker house. you can build this design for whatever woodpecker is common in your area.

The materials list for this house is shown in Fig. 7-9. Look it over and then carefully measure and draw out the various parts on your wood. Try to get all the pieces square so they will fit together nicely. Cut out the roof piece, sand it lightly, and set it aside. Cut the bottom and sides next. Go ahead and drill the drain holes in the bottom and the vent holes in the top of the side pieces. The vent holes should be bored at a slightly upward angle so that

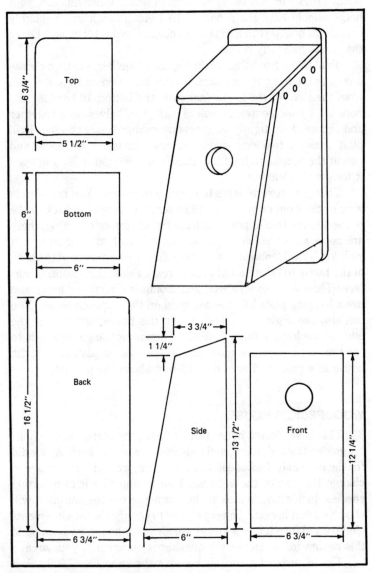

Fig. 7-8. Plan for the woodpecker house.

- 3/8-inch plywood.
- Adhesive or glue (optional).
- 3/4-inch or 1-inch finishing nails or small screws (minimum of 30).
- Silicone bathtub caulk-type adhesive.
- 2 small turnbuttons or similar fasteners.
- Paint or other finish as desired.

Fig. 7-9. Materials list for the woodpecker house.

rain cannot drip in easily. Sand these three pieces, too, and lay them aside. Cut out the back and front pieces now, and cut the 2-inch entrance hole (1 1/2-inch hole for the hairy woodpecker) 9 inches up from the bottom of the front. Sand them lightly. With all the pieces ready, the house is ready for assembly.

Begin by standing one of the side pieces on its *back* edge and running a bead of adhesive along the front edge. Trial fit, and then nail on the front piece. Slip the other side piece into position, glue it, and attach it, too. At this point you will have a front with both sides attached. Lay the unit, front down, and apply glue to the back edges of the side pieces. Center the back piece over them, and nail it on snugly. Turn the house over and attach the roof. I like to use silicone sealant for this job as it is strong and gives the roof real waterproofing.

The bottom piece is all that remains. Trail fit it and do any trimming or sanding necessary to make it fit. Hinge it to the house back, and put two turn buttons in the bottom edge of the front piece to hold the bottom in. Go over the entire house with sandpaper, and then give it a weatherproofing coat of paint or varnish. Let it set for a couple of weeks, and then install it at 12 to 20 feet above the ground.

## EIGHT-FAMILY MARTIN HOUSE

This multifamily house, shown in Figs. 7-10, 7-11, and 7-12, is not an easy project for a first-time builder, but it has been designed to be as simple to build as possible. One of its best features is the way one entire side swings open for cleaning. It allows you to remove the apartment dividers and give the house a good cleaning without having to reach inside eight individual cubbyholes. If you live in martin country, you will want to try one of these.

Look over the list of materials (Fig. 7-13) and gather everything

**129**

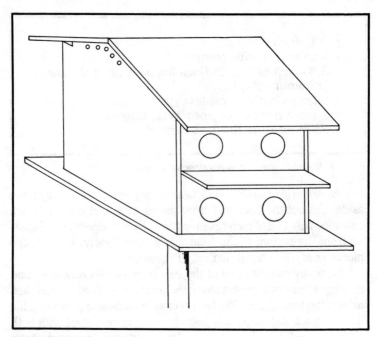

Fig. 7-10. Eight-family martin house.

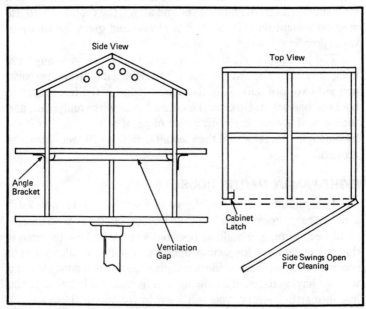

Side View

Top View

Angle
Bracket

Ventilation
Gap

Cabinet
Latch

Side Swings Open
For Cleaning

Fig. 7-11. Side and top views of the eight-family martin house.

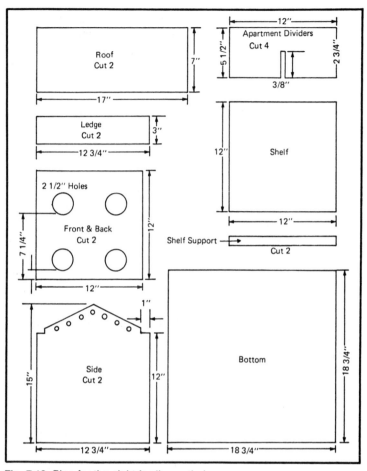

Fig. 7-12. Plan for the eight-family martin house.

- 3/8-inch plywood.
- 3/4-inch or 1-inch nails and /or small screws (minimum of 40).
- Adhesive or glue (optional).
- 2 feet of quarter round stock.
- 2 medium sized hinges.
- Four 2-inch metal angle brackets.
- Cabinet latch or similar fasteners.
- Pipe flange for pipe mounting the house.
- Primer (optional) and white paint for finishing.

Fig. 7-13. Materials list for the eight-family martin house.

you will need for the project. Begin by drawing out all the pieces on your wood. Cut out the roof and ledge pieces, the shelf, and the bottom. Sand the edges of each piece and lay them aside. Cut the four 12 by 5 1/2-inch apartment dividers. Measure and draw centerlines across each at the 6-inch point. Then measure up the centerlines to 2 3/4 inches and make a heavy mark. You will center your 3/8 inch slit on the line and make it as deep as the mark. When you mark and cut all four dividers, put them together. To do this, take one divider and stand it slit up. Slip another, crosswise and slit down, over it until they fit flush together. Do the same with the other two dividers and lay them aside.

Cut out the two side pieces now, and drill the vent holes at the top of each. Cut out the front and back, measure for the entrance holes, and cut them out, too. Find your quarter-round stock and cut the two shelf supports from it. Go over all these pieces with rough sandpaper and get ready for the actual assembly.

The first step will be to join the shelf supports to the front and back pieces. Measure up 6 inches from the bottom of the inside of the front piece and draw a line. Lay one of the shelf supports in place along the line and glue and nail or screw through the supports and into the front piece. Attach the other shelf support to the back piece in the same way.

Measure in 3 inches on all four sides of the bottom piece and draw lines. These will mark the placement of the front, back, and sides and will allow for the 3-inch landing ledge. Lay the front piece on your work table so that it faces you. Mark the left and right sides of it to help remind you as you go. Now stand the front piece on its right side edge. Carefully fit the left side piece over it and glue and nail or screw through the side and into the front piece. Slip the back piece into position and attach it, too. Then turn the unit over and fit and attach the right side, but make this one a temporary installation by tacking it on with small nails. Leave about 1/4 inch of the nails sticking out so you can pull them out when it is time to hinge the side. Watch to be sure that the shelf supports are inside the house and that the edges of the bottom and top are flush with no overlap.

Trial fit the roof sections now, allowing for the overhang and beveling the peak edges as needed to give them a neat fit. Small gaps will be easily filled with silicone bathtub caulk-type adhesive. Drill pilot holes through the roof panels and into the back and front pieces as well as the left side piece (the one that will *not* be hinged). Glue and screw the roof to these pieces with 1-inch screws. Turn the house upside down and line up the bottom piece over it. Drill pilot holes and glue and screw it on, but once again, do not screw it to the right side because that will be hinged.

The basic shell of the house is complete now. Time for finishing touches. Pull out the temporary nails and hinge the right side piece to turn it into a large door. Install a good, strong cabinet latch or hook and eye to keep it closed. Often two latches or hooks are better in case the door warps in the weather. Open the door wide and insert the shelf. Then put one set of apartment dividers on the first floor and the other upstairs. The ledges fit in place 6 inches from the bottom on the front and back. Screw them in place securely using two angle brackets per side as shown in Fig. 7-11. Tip the house over and drill several 1/4-inch drain holes in the bottom.

Because successful martin houses are out in the open and 15 to 20 feet high, they are usually exposed to the full heat of the summer sun. For this reason, white is the only color I can recommend for painting them. Use your favorite priming and sealing method, give the house a couple of coats of white, recheck the drain holes to be sure they have not been sealed by the paint, and you are finished. All that remains is mounting. Install your standard pipe flange on the bottom, and mount it according to the suggestions earlier in the chapter.

## BLUEBIRD CHALET

Although if your aim is to set up a bluebird trail of many bluebird houses, you might want to choose the simple box design. This one (Fig. 7-14) is attractive and novel. The overlapped roof pieces give it good ventilation. Because the entire roof is removable, it is a snap to clean and maintain. The materials list (Fig. 7-15) shows that it can be built inexpensively, too.

This design has several more pieces than the others, so you will need to be careful when laying it out. Check to be sure you have a front and a back, two sides, a hanging plate, a bottom, and six roof pieces. The cutting is straightforward with no tricky measurements or angles to contend with. After you get all the pieces cut, go ahead and drill the drain holes in the bottom piece and bore the 1 1/2-inch entrance hole in the front piece. Sand all the parts lightly and get ready to assemble the house.

Locate the bottom piece and stand it on edge. Glue and nail the front piece on carefully. Next, center the back piece over the hanging plate and screw it on securely. Once this is done, stand the house on the front and glue and nail the back-and-hanger piece

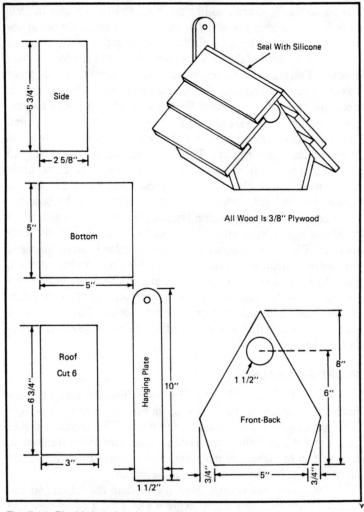

Side — 5 3/4" — 2 5/8"

Bottom — 5" — 5"

Roof Cut 6 — 6 3/4" — 3"

Hanging Plate — 10" — 1 1/2"

Seal With Silicone

All Wood Is 3/8" Plywood

Front-Back — 1 1/2" — 8" — 6" — 3/4" — 5" — 3/4"

Fig. 7-14. Bluebird chalet plan.

on. The sides come next. Fit them in place on either side. Glue and nail them securely to the bottom, front, and back pieces. You should have a house that is complete except for a roof.

This roof is build differently from roofs on the other designs in this book. Start by laying one roof piece down and overlapping another lengthwise over it so that the second piece overlaps the first one by 3/4 inch. Silicone sealant will actually hold the pieces together, so spread a good amount of the sealant on the overlapp-

**134**

- 3/8-inch plywood.
- 3/4-inch finishing nails and/or small screws (minimum of 30).
- Silicone bathtub caulk-type adhesive.
- 1/2-inch tacks.
- Paint, stain, varnish, etc., as desired.

Fig. 7-15. Bluebird chalet materials list.

ing surfaces and fit them together. Then use 1/2-inch or 3/4-inch tacks along the overlap. The tacks will add strength, but they are mainly to hold the structure together so we can continue working without waiting for the silicone sealant to dry. Take a third roof piece and overlap the second one by 3/4 inch in the same way you just did and attach it. You should now have a roof panel with three leaves that measures 7 1/2 inches. Use the other three roof pieces to build the other panel exactly the same way.

Now that you have both roof panels built, trail fit them onto the house. You will see that the panels do not rest flush against the top of the house. They are not supposed to. They were designed for good summer ventilation as well as ease of construction. Match the two peak ends of the panels snugly against each other, but do not overlap them. Judge where the side pieces pass under the roof panels and drill pilot holes down through the roof panel into the side piece in two places on each side. Lift the roof panels and lay a small piece of plastic wrap or aluminum foil over the peaks on the front and back pieces to keep the silicone sealant from sticking to them. Refit the panels again, matching their peak edges snugly and lining up the pilot holes. When you are satisfied with the fit, screw the roof panels down. Do not overtighten the screws or you may cause the peak end to shift. Run a generous and neat bead of silicone sealant all along the roof joint. Be sure to force some of it well down into the joint. It will take several hours for the sealant to cure.

When you are certain the silicone is cured, unscrew the four wood screws and gently lift off the roof. The silicone is strong but yet will pull off with rough use. Turn the roof section over and run another good bead along the inside of the joint. Reinstall the roof leaving the plastic wrap or aluminum foil in place over the front and back pieces, and let it cure again. This time when you remove the roof section, you will find it much stronger. It will bear up quite well over the years as it is removed for cleaning and replaced. All that remains now is to give the whole house a nice sanding and a good weatherproofing coat of varnish or paint. Then, after it airs for a couple of weeks, install it 5 to 10 feet above the ground either on a post or in a tree.

## BLUEBIRD TRAIL BOX HOUSE

This very basic design (Fig. 7-16) is a proven one that is easy

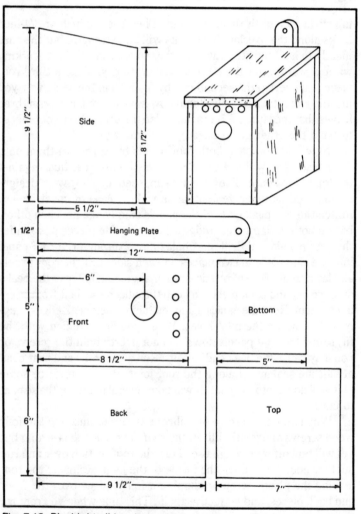

Fig. 7-16. Bluebird trail box house plan.

- 1 cedar, cypress, or redwood fence board (6 feet long 1/2inch by 6 inches wide).
- 1- inch finishing nails and /or screws (minimum of 30).
- Adhesive or glue (optional).
- 2 small hinges.
- 1 small hook and eye or similar fastener.

Fig. 7-17. List of materials for the bluebird trail box house.

and fast to build. It is a favorite of people who put up "bluebird trials" of 6 to 12 or more houses. It can also be used by clubs and Scouts for group projects. As you can see from the materials list (Fig. 7-17), I am specifying the use of redwood or cypress fence panels for this one, because these woods give a natural, rough, weatherproof house without the need for paint or varnish. All it takes is one 6-inch-by-6-foot fence board 1/2 inch thick for the project. Locally the cost is less than $2 from lumber or fencing supply houses.

Cutting out this house is simple and quick. Just draw out all the dimensions using a square and cut them out. Touch each piece up with rough sandpaper and go ahead and drill the drain holes in the bottom piece. Measure up 6 inches from the bottom of the front piece and mark the center for the 1 1/2-inch entrance hole. Use a hole saw to bore the entrance hole or drill a starter hole and then cut it out with a coping saw or jigsaw. While you are working on the front piece, go ahead and bore several 3/8-inch vent holes about 3/4 inch down from the top. These will be under the roof overhang when the house is completed.

Begin the actual assembly by standing the front piece on its top edge and gluing and nailing the bottom on. Be sure you are keeping the entrance hole at the top of the house. Then carefully turn it on its side and attach one of the side pieces to both the bottom piece and the front. Repeat the process for the other side piece. Next, begin work on the back piece by centering it over the hanging plate and screwing several screws through it and into the hanger. Lay the house on its front and position the back piece over it. Glue and nail it securely in place and turn the house right-side-up again.

All that remains is to install the roof. Hinge it to the back of the house and place a quick hook and eye fastener on the front to hold it down. Your bluebird box is ready to put up for occupancy either mounted on a post or to a tree. Bluebirds like to nest 5 to 10 feet above the round, and they prefer an environment of open fields with nearby woods.

## ESTABLISHING YOUR OWN BLUEBIRD TRAIL

One of America's most popular birds, the bluebird, was in serious trouble only a very few years ago and still is in some parts of the country. Once a very common sight in suburban and rural areas, a three-punch combination caused it to very nearly disappear in many areas across the country. The first culprit was a series of unusually rough winters. These winters in the 50s were so severe that scientists estimated that perhaps as much as one half of the entire bluebird population was wiped out. (Another argument for well-stocked bird feeders!) In the few years after, concerned bird hobbyists and conservationists saw that the bluebird was not making the kind of quick increase needed to build the population back up. In fact, it seemed that each year they counted fewer birds than before. By the early 60s there were fewer bluebirds than at any other point in history.

When the hobbyists and conservationists got serious and studied the plight of the Eastern bluebird, they uncovered the other two contributing factors. The first had to do with the birds' nesting habits. Bluebirds do not nest in bushes and trees as most common songbirds do. They are hole-nesters taking over unoccupied holes hollowed out by woodpeckers or other birds and animals. It turned out that there was a housing shortage at the time. The natural habitat simply didn't supply enough holes for all the birds that preferred them. The timid bluebirds were being forced out of nesting sites by woodpeckers, sparrows, wrens, and other birds. Why, after all this time, were the bluebirds suddenly unable to find nesting sites? It was pathetically easy to answer. The bluebirds were suffering from an almost total destruction of their natural habitat.

An ideal bluebird habitat is one with old, established woods and orchards. The trees will have old, gnarled branches with generations of woodpecker holes in them, enough to accommodate both bluebirds and the other hole-nesters around. Open grassland, providing good insect hunting, will be near, but farm houses and subdivisions, where sparrows tend to congregate, will be far away. Unfortunately, a habitat like this is rare in the 70s and 80s. Farmers have sold off their acreage or at very least removed the old, unprofitable trees with their ideal nesting holes and put in a new crop.

Subdivisions are everywhere and so are the sparrows that compete with the bluebirds for food, water, and nesting sites.

Once the bluebird's problems became public, many people got involved in the solution. The most common approach, and the most successful, that came out of all the research and trial-and-error was the bluebird trail. The idea was to provide nesting sites to take the place of the natural ones lost. Many people and several government agencies could be named as pioneers or perfectors, but over the years the differences have been ironed out and a basic plan for a bluebird trail remains.

To start your own bluebird trail, spend the winter making eight to ten (or more) simple bluebird nesting boxes. There are many different styles and designs, including the bluebird chalet and bluebird trail box house in this chapter. All will do quite nicely as long as they adhere to the basic size recommendations. Because you will have to make so many, I suggest a simple design. In the long run, the birds don't care whether it is plain or fancy. Make your houses of weatherproof woods like redwood, cedar, or cypress, or use several coats or paint or varnish to coat them. After all the work of building them, you certainly want them to last more than one season.

If you are a member of a club you may want to involve other people in a group project. Boy Scouts, bird watchers' clubs, senior citizens, and Sunday school groups often get together and build the houses and cosponsor a bluebird trail. It gives a real sense of accomplishment.

During the winter while you are building your bluebird houses do a little scouting to find a likely place to establish your trail. You will want a place convenient to your home so you can check on the birds and houses frequently. You will be looking for a place with both woods and open fields or pastures if possible. You will want to find out if you will be able to attach your houses to existing posts or poles or if you will have to place your own posts. Often a farmer will be happy to allow you to nail or wire houses to his pasture fences once he knows your purpose, and especially if he understands that bluebirds do great service ridding his land of insects. Power companies will usually allow you to nail houses to their poles, too, after you call and explain your intent. Finally, choose whether you want a circular, looping route between houses and back to the start point or a one way, here-to-there trail, and lay it out in your mind.

When March arrives, it is time to set up the trail. Take along wire, wire cutters, nails and hammer, etc., along with posts if you will need them. Be sure you have permission before you start out nailing your houses to other people's property. Set your houses 500 to 1000 feet apart and only 3 to 4 feet off the ground. Experience has shown that sparrows are very unlikely to take over nesting boxes that are lower than 5 feet from the ground. Nail them on securely or use wire to fasten them to metal fence posts. Tack a notecard, protected by a bit of plastic, to each house explaining the purpose of the house and whom to contact in case of damage. This usually helps to limit wanton vandalism. Travel the length of your trail placing your nesting boxes. Then retrace your steps and give them a final look to see if you have forgotten anything.

Several years ago some local bird lovers developed a bluebird trail that should provide a good example. It covered just about every type of terrain in the area. They started about three quarters of a mile outside their city putting out 2-by-4-foot posts and a nesting box every 500 feet or so along the highway back against the trees. After placing nine boxes, they veered off into a low, swampy area, found a clear spot a few yards from a creek, and put two boxes there, one on either side of the creek. They did not put any houses on trees because posts have proven to be more attractive to bluebirds for some reason. On the other side of the creek was about a quarter-mile of thick woods where they did not place a house, and then open pasture land dotted with clumps of trees. Here they had permission from the rancher to wire the nesting boxes onto his steel fenceposts. They placed nine more boxes along the pasture edge. The boxes are wired on the outside side of the fence, by the way, so that they are easy to clean and service without climbing through the fence. In all, they placed 20 houses along their 2 1/2 mile trail.

This club planned ahead so that the trail would not be a burden to supervise and maintain. All the houses are within view from the highway so that the builders can see if any are damaged by storms or vandals. Individual houses are easy to check that way, too. Then once every week or two weeks, one of the members of the club hikes along the entire length of the trail and notes the condition and occupancy of the houses. In the fall it is a group project to clean and close up the houses to keep them ready for next spring. The trail is six years old now and still thriving with about 75 percent of the houses occupied each year.

# Chapter 8

# Projects for Kids

**B**IRDS FASCINATE KIDS. IT IS A NATURAL FACT. YOU CAN DE-
light a child by showing him a brightly colored bird or letting
him feed ducks in the park. I think part of the reason is that birds
are so beautiful and so familiar in kids' lives, but there are the
mysteries of flight and nesting, too. No matter how much information a child has picked up about birds, he is still amazed by their
beauty and habits. Kids are so eager to learn that if another person around them is involved in feeding or attracting birds, they are
bound to want a part in it, too.

You can involve kids in the hobby as much or as little as you
wish. Some people are happiest just allowing the kids to help out
filling the feeder from time to time or cleaning birdhouses occasionally. Others work on building responsibility by assigning chores
like stocking the feeder on a regular basis. Building feeders or
houses can be great family projects especially if they are simple
enough to allow the child real hands-on participation. (Busywork
is quickly recognized and not popular.) Older children can learn a
lot about using tools, measuring, and simple construction if
allowed to build a project on their own with supportive adult
guidance.

Children need to be aware that attracting birds has a useful
purpose in addition to being fun. It is never too early to start building
concern for animals and the environment. Even small children are
amazingly compassionate. Winter feeding and providing houses for

nesting are activities that give children a strong feeling that they are doing something to help birds.

My favorite projects for kids are short and simple enough for the child to do most—if not all—of the work. For younger children it might be helpful if an older person "kits" the project first. This means to gather all the materials, cut out the parts, do the drilling, etc. In other words, have everything laid out so that the child can assemble the project with a huge chance of total success. For older children, a little gentle guidance as they learn to measure and use tools teaches them a lot. The main idea here is to keep it a "fun" and "low pressure" activity. If you are going to expect a 9-year-old child to be able to drive a nail straight or an 11-year-old to be able to join perfect right-angle corners, please don't get involved. It will mean frustration for you and the child. The birds don't care if the corners match or the paint is runny or not. Give the child the thrill of constructing a finished project, perfect or not, and hang it or use it with pride. If you make a positive experience out of the project, you have gained much more than a crooked feeder shows.

## PINECONE FEEDER

This is an old idea that never fails or falls out of fashion. It is easy enough so that most 5-year-old children can do it with a little help, and it has been a favorite project for schools, Sunday school, and Scouts for years.

For young children, the hunt for a good pinecone can be an adventure by itself. Any pinecone will work, but the larger, more open ones are best. Here in the South we have huge pinecones that come off the long-leaf pines. Some of them measure 6 to 8 inches, and their open structure leaves lots of room for stuffing with bird-food. When you have found your pinecone, give it a good shaking and tapping to remove loose pieces and any insects that might be hiding inside. Then take a long piece of yarn and run it around the pinecone, pulling it tight inside just below the stem end. Tie a knot snugly in place. The yarn will be your hanger.

Filling the pinecone feeder is messy fun. The simplest filler consists of peanut butter and seed food. Just scoop some peanut butter out into a shallow pan and roll the pinecone around in it, pressing to force plenty of peanut butter up into the spaces between the "leaves." When you are finished, pour out some of the seed food and do the same thing, getting a thick, even coating over the entire surface. Shake off the excess seed. You are ready to hang the feeder.

I like to hang this feeder nearby where the child can watch it and see the birds using it. The birds find these feeders quickly and peck them clean. The kids are delighted, and they can take the pinecone down and refill it.

## TREEFOOD RECIPES

Treefood is thick, mixed food usually offered by smearing it onto the limbs and trunks of trees. It is also great for filling pinecone feeders or suet logs. It is a favorite of many bird lovers, and, of course, many varieties of birds, too. Treefood is excellent winter food because its base is usually a fat food, good for providing lots of energy on cold days. Although most bird lovers serve treefood right in their yards, some also establish regular treefood feeding stations in nearby woods. They simply make a trip along their trail once or twice a week and smear treefood onto branches along the way. The wild birds quickly get used to the new food supply. Treefood trails are excellent ways of providing winter food for birds that are too shy to visit your yard.

There are dozens of recipes for treefood. In fact, almost every serious bird feeder has customized his or her own favorite. These two are easy. Children, especially older ones, should be able to tackle either of them with little help.

### PEANUT BUTTER BASED TREEFOOD
1 cup peanut butter (smooth or chunky)
1/2 cup bread or cracker crumbs
1/4 cup crushed dog meal
1/2 cup millet or other bird seed

Simply mix all the ingredients together, and the mix is ready to smear on tree limbs or trunks. Peanut butter varies as to thickness, so it is often necessary to vary these proportions slightly. It may be necessary to add more seed or bread crumbs if your peanut butter is on the thin side. (You want it thick enough to stay on the branches or tree trunk.) Remember that if you serve treefood outside in cold weather, it will stiffen as it gets chilled.

### SUET BASED TREEFOOD
2 cups twice-melted suet
1 cup seed mix
1/2 cup sunflower seeds
1 package mosquito larvae, ant eggs, tubifex worms, etc., from aquarium store

This recipe is a real favorite of insectivores. Chop and melt the suet over medium heat. Then allow it to cool completely and remelt it. This gives you a smoother, harder, more consistent suet. While it is still warm, mix in the other ingredients a little of each at a time until you have a rather stiff mixture. Because suet and the other ingredients vary so much, you might end up leaving out part of the dry ingredients or adding more to get a good stiff mixture. Remember that as the mixture gets chilled outside in cold weather, it will become very stiff and adhere to branches and trunks very well. I don't recommend using suet based treefood in the warmer months because it does melt. It is mainly a winter food.

## BIRD FOOD GARLANDS

Small children always enjoy helping the wild birds around them, and making bird food garlands is one of the easiest and most gratifying ways for them to do it. The materials for the garlands are easy to come by, inexpensive, and familiar to children. The process of making the garlands is one that is enjoyable and at the same time is good motor skills practice for small hands. If several members of a family or class get together and string garlands, it can be enjoyable, social pastime, with fun sharing the work, snacking, and visiting. In my family, making garlands is a good way to spend a cold winter Saturday afternoon together.

You can make bird food garlands out of any foods that can reasonably be strung on heavy thread or cord. Favorites are popcorn, bread balls, apple slices, raisins, semimoist dog food chunks, boiled potato chunks, and elbow macaroni cooked just barely tender. If you know of any other foods that will string and stay on the string over a period of a week or so, try them. This is an area where knowledge of your local birds will help you decide what to use. If you have tried table scraps in your feeders and found that your birds leave them, naturally you won't include scraps in your plans for garland making. Stick instead to popcorn (always a favorite and cheap), bread balls, and fruit, depending heaviest on the popcorn.

Once you have decided on the ingredients to use, prepare them and lay them out on paper plates or in bowls. Popcorn must be popped, of course, and apples or oranges sliced. To prepare bread balls, cut the crust from sandwich-style white bread, fresh and spongy, and squeeze and knead each slice into a solid lump. Cut each one into balls about the size of walnuts and squeeze them round and solid. Get everything laid out within easy reach of the garland makers.

For the actual stringing, begin by threading a large needle with monofilament fishing line, upholstery thread, or other strong cord. Don't use regular thread, because as the birds peck at the foods strung on it, they will inadvertently break it. Tie an old button at the end of the the the thread for the strung food to butt up against to prevent it from simply working its way over and off the knot. Thread some popcorn, then begin alternating occasional chunks of dog food, raisins, bread balls, or chunks of fruit. When you thread fruit, it is important to thread through the skin of apples or through the membrane of the orange sections; otherwise, one or two good pecks will cause them to fall off the garland. Make the garland as long as you care to or have each person work on his own and tie them together when complete.

Making a bird food garland can be tedious for young children. Stringing the foods is a hard job involving a lot of hand-eye coordination from them. They will get tired after only a foot or less of garland. I try not to put any length requirements on younger children, and try to make it as much fun and as positive an experience as possible. They will be proud of their garland, even if it is only a few inches long. They will feel better stopping there if they are tired than if they have to go on with it.

Older children usually see garland stringing as a social event. They often get involved in friendly rivalries and try to string the longest garland or divide up into teams and work together. They also enjoy snacking as they work, so salt the popcorn and have the fruit washed and ready to eat. Just like stringing popcorn for the Christmas tree, it will be string a few, eat a few, all day.

Once you have a garland ready, it is a simple matter to drape it across low branches or bushes for the birds to find. I like to choose a spot where the children who worked on the garland can see it and watch the birds enjoy it. Secure it well enough so that wind does not blow it off the tree or bush, and avoid having it bridge long expanses between branches or bushes where the birds won't have good access to it. If you have maintained a feeding station in your yard and have a group of regular bird visitors, you will find that birds will begin to enjoy your garland right away. If not, it might take a few days, but soon enough birds will be pecking away at it.

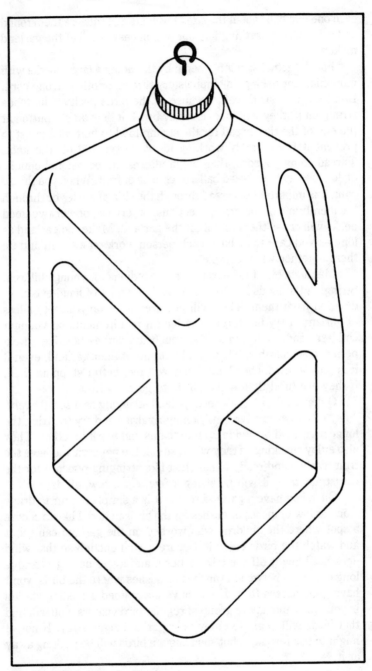

Fig. 8-1. Milk jug tray feeder plan.

## MILK JUG TRAY FEEDER

The milk jug tray feeder, shown in fig. 8-1, is another project that can be completed in about half an hour. It is easy, inexpensive, and reliable. A child who can handle a knife and scissors can do this one on his own if there is someone around to drill the one hole required.

Begin this project by washing out a 1-gallon milk jug. You will need the cap, too, so wash it and save it. For cutting out the sides of the jug, you will need a sharp knife and maybe scissors. If you look at the jug, you will see that it has two relatively flat sides and two that are molded inward to allow for handles. Begin cutting by measuring 1 1/2 inches up from the bottom of the jug on one of the flat sides. Mark the line and cut a slit along it. Be careful *not* to cut closer than 1 inch from either corner. Turn the knife or scissors and make a cut up the side of the jug, still not cutting closer than 1 inch from the corner. When you get to where the jug begins to curve inward at the top, stop, remove your knife or scissors, and cut a slit up the other side the same way. Once this is done, you merely have to join the slits across the top and remove the cut out piece of plastic. Do the same on the other flat side and on the handle sides, too, except that there you must make the cutouts much shorter to clear the handle. All that remains is to drill a hole in the cap, bolt an eyebolt through it, and screw the cap on very tightly. The feeder is now ready to fill with any type of birdfood and hang out for the birds.

## SIMPLE SPARROW OR WREN HOUSE

This very simple house, shown in Fig. 8-2, is made from a 1/2-gallon plastic jug, the type that chocolate milk or juice comes in. Any other jug of about the same size will do as well.

Wash out a 1/2-gallon plastic jug and cut it in two just below the base of the handle. You will end up with a top portion including the neck of the jug and a longer bottom section. Trim this longer section a little bit at a time until when you fit it back to the neck section, the two pieces together measure 7 inches from the neck to the bottom. Now trim the neck of the jug a little at a time until the opening (not the outer measurement) is 1 1/4 inches in diameter. Once that is finished, find a piece of scrap wood an inch or two longer than the width of the bottom of the jug. You will use this board to nail or tie through when you mount the house. Stand the jug bottom on the wood so that when seen from above, the handle

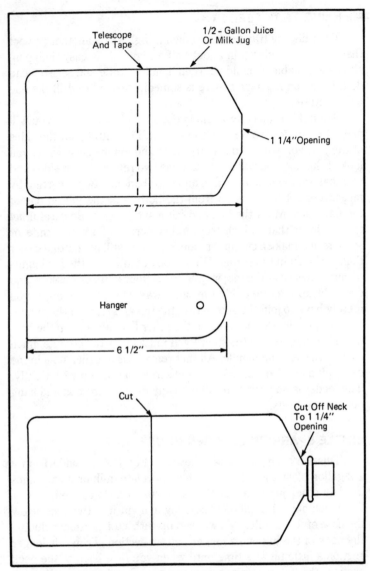

Fig. 8-2. Plan for simple sparrow or wren house.

is facing right and the board's extra length is sticking out the top. Tack through the jug bottom and into the wood to hold it on securely. Fit the two sections together again and tape them snugly together with wide, weatherproof tape like duct tape. Use plenty, both to hold it together and to provide support for the thin plastic.

I like to use brown or green duct-type tape to make a house look natural. I also like to add a perch, a piece of dowel wood that sticks out past the opening of the house several inches. The easy way to attach it is to hold it in place and wrap several snug turns of duct tape around it—the same way you put the house itself together. Sparrows especially appreciate a perch. Then nail or tie the house to a tree in a shady place. It is important to choose a shady location because plastic is not a good insulator, and the house will get very hot in the sun.

## NESTING MATERIALS RACK

Nesting materials can be very hard for birds to find in urban

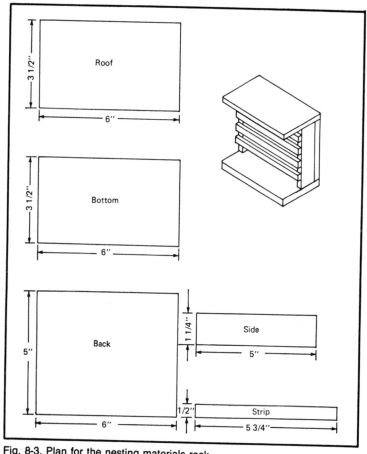

Fig. 8-3. Plan for the nesting materials rack.

- 3/8-inch plywood
- 3/4-inch or 1-inch finishing nails.
- Adhesive or glue for joints (optional).
- Strong, weatherproof adhesive (epoxy, silicone bathtub caulk-type adhesive, etc.) or small paneling nails for attaching front strips.
- 3-inch angle bracket.
- Paint or other finish as desired.

Fig. 8-4. List of materials for the nesting materials rack.

areas. Providing fabric scraps, yarn, straw, lint from the dryer, and other materials is helpful and will attract birds to your yard. This rack, shown in Fig. 8-3, gives a place to supply them. The measuring, cutting, and assembly are pretty simple. This might be a good project to "kit" for a child and then give him guidance as he assembles it.

Look over the materials list for this project (Fig. 8-4) to be sure you have everything you need to build it. Then measure and draw out the bottom, roof, back, and two side pieces. Cut them out carefully and sand them lightly. The rack strips are made of the same 3/8-inch plywood. Cut them into strips 1/2 inch wide. You should cut a long 1/2-inch strip (or two) and then cut out four of the 5 3/4-inch rack strips from it. Sand these, too, and get ready to put the rack together.

The first step will be to lay one of the side pieces on its long edge, lay the back piece over it, line it up flush, and glue and nail through the back pieces and into it. Do the same on the other side to end up with a back with two side pieces attached. Stand this unit up, trial fit the bottom piece and attach it, gluing and nailing through the bottom and into the back and sides. Attach the roof in the same way. The rack strips come next. Squeeze a dollop of silicone adhesive onto each end of each strip and, with the rack itself lying on its back, glue them on between the side pieces. If you prefer, you can nail the strips on with small finishing nails. Try to have them fairly evenly spaced and fairly straight. Set the rack aside while the adhesive dries. Once it has cured, you can sand the whole rack and paint or varnish it as you please. Then screw the angle bracket in place in the middle of the top or bottom of the rack with the angle even with the back edge. Mount it to a post, fence, tree, or other upright surface. (You could also mount it on a pipe if you install a pipe flange on the bottom.) Stuff nesting materials through the rack strips and let the birds have their pick.

## BERRY BASKETS AS NESTING MATERIALS RACKS

One of the simplest and least expensive projects is this suggestion for using a plastic strawberry basket to offer nesting materials to your birds in the spring. The only materials needed are a berry basket and some strong cord. Monofilament or nylon cord lasts longest outside, but any type that is strong enough will do fine. If you don't have a berry basket handy, and small wicker or wire basket will do. Just be sure it has an open weave to allow for good drainage of rain.

Wash the berry basket and allow it to dry while you accumulate the nesting materials to fill it. A brief list of nesting materials would include raveled string or rope, yarn, thin strips of woven fabric, Spanish moss, pulled-apart cotton balls, tufts of polyester pillow filling, and cut bristles from a paint brush. Actually any material light and flexible enough to be woven into their nests will be used by the birds. Because so many of their natural nesting materials (like horsehair) are no longer commonly available, birds have become very adaptable.

Find a suitable spot to place your basket as safe as possible from dogs and cats and in a place where you will be able to watch the birds as they visit it. Be sure you don't choose too high a location, or you will need a ladder to fill it. Once you are satisfied with the spot, weave the cord through the basket a couple of times, wrap it around the tree trunk or post, and tie it securely. All that is left is to fill it part way full with your nesting materials and let the birds take their pick. I like to have nesting materials available from April to September—throughout the nesting season.

## NESTING SHELF

Many types of birds prefer to nest on open shelves. Figure 8-5 is sized to meet the requirements of phoebes, song sparrows, and some types of swallows, but I have had robins use them, too. Nesting shelves are good to have in addition to standard houses, because they attract a different set of birds.

There are just five pieces to cut out for this project counting the two sides. Look at the list of materials (Fig. 8-6) for the thickness of wood needed. Then carefully measure and draw out each shape. To draw the cut-in for the two side pieces, first measure 1 inch

from the top and from the bottom of the front edge of each side
piece. Mark those spots heavily. Then measure 3 inches up from
the bottom edge of each piece at the front edge and again near the
middle. Mark these spots and draw a line between them. Measure
3 inches in from the front along this line and place a dark mark.
All that remains is to use a straight edge to join the 1 inch marks

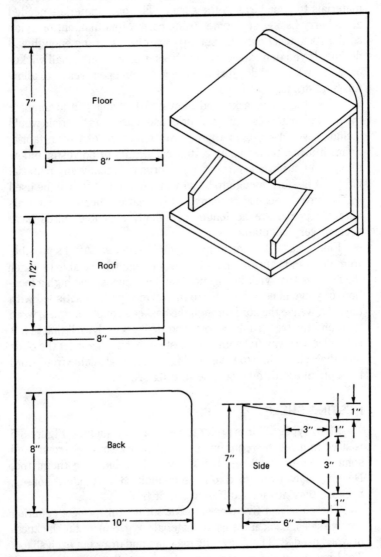

Fig. 8-5. Nesting shelf plan.

- 3/8 inch plywood.
- Adhesive or glue (optional).
- 3/4-inch or 1-inch finishing nails or small screws (minimum of 25).
- 1/4-inch dowel scrap or other scrap wood for nest anchors.
- Paint or finish as desired.

Fig. 8-6. Materials list for the nesting shelf.

on the edge to this last mark you made. The easiest way to round the top corners of the back piece is simply to find something round of the right size, lay it over the corners, and trace it. I usually go through the kitchen until I find a can of the proper diameter and use it. Once you have all the pieces cut out, buff them with sandpaper until they have no rough edges. You are ready to put the shelf together.

To begin, first measure and draw a line on the back piece that is 1 1/8 inches from the bottom. This will mark where the bottom of the two sides fit. Now mark two other lines, one on each side, 1/2 inch in from the side edges. This will line up the full length of the side pieces. Stand one of the side pieces on its front edge and place the back piece over it. Line it up so that the side piece meets the 1/2-inch line along the side edge and the 1 1/8-inch line at the bottom. Glue and nail through the back and into the side piece. Slip the other side piece into position and attach it, too. You will put the floor on next, so stand the unit upside down so that it rests on the top (roof) edges of the two side pieces. You will see that it is awkward because the back is too long to allow it to lay flat. Solve that by moving it to the edge of a table where the back piece can hang over. Fit the floor in place and glue and nail it. Turn the shelf over, hang it over the table edge again to allow for the bottom of the back piece, and glue and nail the roof on.

There is not much left to this project now. One thing, however, that many shelf designs leave out is nest anchors. Too many times nests are blown or tipped out of nesting shelves because there is no rail or other means to keep them in. You can make nest anchors by simply drilling the floor and installing about 4 pieces of 1/4-inch dowel about 1 inch long or by just gluing or tacking strips of wood about 1/2 inch thick across the front about 1 inch in from the edge. Don't completely close the front edge, though. It has to be open for good drainage. When your nest anchors are in place, paint or varnish the shelf as you like, and mount it at a height of 8 to 12 feet. Be careful not to mount it where it will be directly in the afternoon sun or where it will be exposed to the sun all day.

# Index

# Index

Edited by Jodi L. Tyler